A Private's Diary
The World War I Diary of Robert W. Safstrom

Chad R. Justesen, MD

Copyright © 2014 Chad R. Justesen, MD

All rights reserved.

ISBN:1502317532
ISBN-13:9781502317537

For my wife Shawn, and for all the men and women who have served their country honorably, during peace and war.

CONTENTS

	Provenance	i
1	Robert W. Safstrom Biography	1
2	Entering The War	5
3	Journey To The Front	19
4	The Front Lines	27
5	The Saint-Mihiel Drive	41
6	Battle of The Argonne	47
7	Wounded In Action	57
8	The Long Trip Home	83
	Notes	95
	Photographs	101
	Letters To Home	105
	Map of Locations	107
	Diary Page Sample	108
	About The Author	109

PROVENANCE

In the fall of 2013 I met with Wanda Justesen Bergh, my aunt, to share photographs and documents related to our family genealogy. As part of that, she brought me a photocopied transcription of the World War I diary of Robert Waldemar Safstrom. Bob was my great-grandmother Hulda's brother, and I was immediately fascinated by his tale, not necessarily for the great writing or heroics, but for the detail and work he put into it. Knowing that most of my Scandinavian relatives are prone to understatement and self-effacement, I read between the lines and felt the emotions of a young man going off to fight a terrible war.

Half a year went by as I worked on other aspects of my family's history, then one night while sitting on the balcony of a bed and breakfast, the sun waning over the horizon, the lake below me still and quiet, I decided that I could not let this work go to waste. Bob obviously put a lot of effort into recording his experience, and not sharing his story with at least a few more people would be a tragedy. This decision, in an irony I did not appreciate until later, came while I was staying in Hankinson, North Dakota, the first train stop on Bob's trip to the war.

Through Wanda I contacted Betty Terriere, Bob's daughter, and asked for her approval and help, to which she readily agreed. She still has the original diary and lent it to me for this book. The initial transcription was done by Bob's son James, now deceased. The photographs in the book were assembled mostly from Wanda and a few from my father's collection. The cover photographs, artwork, and map are mine. Editing for spelling, clarification of place names, and sentence structure was performed. I also added chapter titles and chronologically organized the text. I sincerely thank Betty, Wanda, and my wife Shawn for their help.

C.R.J. 2014

1 ROBERT W. SAFSTROM

A Swedish immigrant, along with his parents and siblings, sixteen year old Robert Waldemar Safstrom settled in Sargent County, North Dakota in 1903. They arrived in New York City aboard the S.S. Hellig Olav, a 500 foot long, 60 foot wide steamship, newly built by Alexander Stephen and Sons from Scotland, that sailed from Copenhagen to Oslo to the United States. She had accommodations for about 270 first and second class passengers, but the Safstrom family likely joined the 1,000 to 1,400 people in third class. The voyage across the Atlantic lasted about 14 days, and was probably a good test of endurance and spirit. The trip to Gwinner, Sargent County, North Dakota was facilitated by the newly completed extension of the Northern Pacific Railroad.

Robert, born near Rullbo, Gävleborg County, Sweden on December 5th, 1887, was the son of Andrew and Anna Marie Safstrom. Andrew operated his own harness and leather shop in Gwinner and lived from 1847 to 1929. Anna Marie lived from 1850 to 1928. Robert had four older siblings; sisters Amanda and Hulda, brothers John and Fridolf; and one younger brother, Hilding. Amanda, whose fiancé in Sweden died in an accident, married John Ek later in life. Hulda married Frank W. Youngberg, owner of an eponymous general store in Gwinner and later Litchville,

North Dakota. John Safstrom came to the United States ahead of the rest of the family, became a minister of the Congregational Church in Gwinner, and died young of a lingering illness. In fact, Robert learned of John's death a few days after his voyage from France to New York City, returning from the war. Fridolf was the manager of a Gwinner lumber yard before he joined his brother-in-law John Ek in the Safstrom & Ek Hardware store. Robert's youngest brother Hilding also served in the Great War in France, later taking jobs as a telegrapher for the Northern Pacific Railroad in Minnesota and North Dakota.

While in school Robert developed a love of math and numbers, and this led to his father's support to attend the American Business School in Minneapolis, Minnesota for training in accounting. When he returned to Gwinner he worked as an accountant for Safstrom & Ek Hardware.

At age 31, on March 29th, 1918, Robert enlisted in the United States Army. He went to Camp Dodge, Iowa for training, and was assigned to Company Q, 4th Battalion, of the 163rd Depot Brigade. Like many recruits trained at Camp Dodge, he was soon reassigned. After three short weeks in Iowa, he was sent to Camp Mills on Long Island where he was transferred to Company M, 138th Regiment, 35th Division, and shipped overseas.

The diary you are about to read starts on his first day in Camp Dodge and continues to his discharge on May 12th, 1919, at Fort Snelling, Minnesota. His story includes his travels from North Dakota to Iowa, New York City, Great Britain, France, and back across the Atlantic through a storm. Wounded by shrapnel to his left shoulder from an exploding shell on September 26th, 1918, on the front lines at Meuse-Argonne, he made his own way, walking past Red Cross stations with no ambulances, to find a hospital with an open bed. Following surgery he spent 67 days at bed rest before starting the long pilgrimage home. He earned his Purple Heart.

While his shoulder injury was serious during the recovery phase in France, mostly due to infections, Robert was discharged with a 25% disability and was able to use his arm fairly normally. He was left with arthritis, some limited mobility, and two divots that looked like a big tablespoon had scraped them out.

After the war, Robert returned to Gwinner and his accounting job at Safstrom & Ek. In 1922 he ran for and won the election for Sargent County Auditor, a position he held continuously until retirement in 1959. An honest, even-tempered, extroverted man, he took his re-election campaigns seriously. As County Auditor he was responsible for assessments, taxes, all the county's financial transactions, apportionment of county and township funds, fishing and hunting licenses, and even hail insurance.

In 1928, at age 41, Robert married Rose Hollstein, a minister at the Congregational Church, and they started a family in Forman. Rose grew up near Frankfort, Illinois in a German immigrant community. When she was in the sixth grade her father sold their dairy farm and moved to Beach, North Dakota. Rose and her family prospered in their cattle raising business, and although her father was reluctant she enrolled in Valley City State Teacher's College, taught school for a couple of years, and then set off for Berkeley College in California. She met Robert in Gwinner, North Dakota, when she was working as a minister in the Congregational Church. They had two daughters, Betty Terriere and Donna Mae Olcott, and a son, James.

Alert and active until the end, Robert died suddenly of heart failure August 30th, 1968 in Sargent County. He went to bed as usual, and his wife heard him give one big cough before he died. Robert, his wife Rose, son James, parents Andrew and Anna Marie, and sisters Amanda Ek and Hulda Youngberg are all buried in Gwinner City Cemetery alongside each other.

Robert W. Safstrom, Camp Dodge, Iowa, April 1918

2 ENTERING THE WAR

Camp Dodge, Iowa to Camp Mills, New York

My first day in Camp Dodge was Easter Sunday, March 31, 1918. We arrived there from home the evening before, or night rather, as it was past midnight when we got to our destination. We had a very good time on our trip. At Hankinson, North Dakota, our special train stopped and we were served a lunch of sandwiches, doughnuts, and coffee by the ladies of the Hankinson Red Cross. Early in the morning we arrived at Fort Snelling in Minneapolis and were marched to the Arcade where we were given breakfast. We ate dinner in the dining car but when we reached Ames, Iowa, we were taken to the First Methodist Church where kind hands had prepared the biggest meal we had seen so far and for an hour we were intensely busy satisfying the cravings of the body. While we ate, a large chorus sang patriotic selections which helped us enjoy ourselves so much more.

From the time we left home until we reached Camp Dodge it was one big celebration. Bands played for us, choirs sang for us, crowds cheered for us, and we started to believe that we were *Some Boys*. On arrival in camp, however, the cheering died down. There was no fuss about us at all. We were very unceremoniously herded into our different barracks after assignment to various companies. The Sargent County boys were put in Company Q, 163rd Depot Brigade, and after eating a late supper we were each given a straw tick and sent to a large shed where they were filled with straw. As soon as we had enough in the ticks we went back to our barracks and rolled in.

The following day, Easter Sunday, we did nothing, with the exception of two boys who were unfortunate enough to be caught spitting on the floor and as punishment had to scrub the stairway the whole day. We felt very sorry for the boys, and were beginning to realize that we were in the army sure enough. A few stragglers who fell by the wayside in Minneapolis and lost the train arrived in the morning, and were promptly locked up in the guardhouse.

The first two weeks we were 'shot' and examined, besides putting in some pretty stiff drilling. If I remember right we received five different shots; three vaccinations and two injections for typhoid. We were examined time and time again. There were two especially strict examinations, one for tuberculosis and the other for the heart.

Measures for our uniforms were taken and in about a week we received our new uniforms. We now settled down to drill, meanwhile getting equipped with the things a soldier needs. All of our officers at Camp Dodge were splendid men who took interest in our welfare and at all times treated us courteously. The first sergeant, however, was a man of low breeding and earned the enmity of every man he came in contact with. An old regular who had seen service in Mexico, the Philippine Islands, and China, he had the deepest contempt for rookies and treated us worse than dogs. He carried a heavy club in the drill field and if a man did not keep step he would use the club to trip him, and for the slightest mistake he would punish a man by 'double timing' for at least a half hour. I do not doubt that he could have been court-martialed for this, in fact one of our officers told us as much, but we were too green at the game to stand up for our rights at that time.

On account of sickness we were under quarantine all the time we were at Camp Dodge. That meant confinement to the company area and we were not even allowed to go to the canteen just across the street. The Y.M.C.A. tried to help us, however, and in the afternoons we would march back to the barracks from the drill field for a 'sing'. We were allowed about fifteen minutes for this. A man from the Y.M.C.A. led the singing and became very popular with us. On Sundays he would come over to our barracks and preach to us. He was one person that we were glad to listen to.

A Bible class and a French school were started but we did not get the benefit of either as we received orders to leave Camp Dodge after only three weeks at that place. The overseas equipment was issued to us late in the evening of the 24th and through a mistake by the clerk, who got my name mixed up with someone who had been rejected for overseas service, no equipment was issued to me. It took a lot of arguing on my part to convince the officer in charge that I was entitled to the equipment. Finally I got my issue and in the morning of April 25th we left Camp Dodge for Camp Mills, Long Island, New York.

The trip to New York was a sequel to the trip from Forman to Camp Dodge. The people were cheering us and waving flags at us the whole trip. At Elkhart, Indiana and Syracuse, New York we paraded through the cities and received splendid ovations. Old Civil War veterans would edge close to us and say "good luck boys, we know what you are up against. We went through it in '61." We passed through Louisville, Kentucky and Chicago, Illinois and in all had a most enjoyable time. With good clean tourist cars we could not help but feel good, although the feed we now were getting was decidedly rotten, what little we got of it, and we were still in the U.S.A.

We arrived in New York on the 28th of April and proceeded by ferry to Long Island where we boarded another train for Camp Mills. Camp Mills was a tent camp, at least I did not see any barracks. The 35th Division was there under orders to sail for France and as they had to be up to full war strength before they could sail, and were somewhat below that, we were transferred to this division. I was put in Company M, 138th Regiment, 35th Division, Kansas and

Missouri National Guards, and was issued the equipment that I still needed. We were given rifles, packs, trench tools, and a lot of other articles. We also had to give up one pair of russet shoes for two pairs of hob nails. Our bundle of equipment was formidable, and our pack and rifle plus the important barracks bag made a load that took a lot of nerve to tackle.

It was very cold and with no stove in our tent we had a hard time keeping warm. The large Mineola Aviation Field was located near the camp and we were much interested in watching the aviators perform, which they did whenever the weather permitted it.

Off to England

In the afternoon of May 1st we left Camp Mills, first by train and then by ferry, and made our way to where the transports to carry us across the Atlantic were waiting. We saw a good many interesting sights while the ferry was lazily making its way from the shores of Long Island to the harbor of New York. Passing under the Brooklyn Bridge and the other large bridges, we had a very good view of the city of New York, with its tall buildings like the Singer, Woolworth, Flatiron, and others.

We passed a large, upturned ocean liner that was one of the transports to go in a convoy to France with soldiers. German spies had either bored holes or opened some portholes which let the water in and tipped the boat over. I don't think any lives were lost, though, as this work of treachery had not been properly executed and the boat turned over before it left the harbor. This was the first scene of German barbarism that we saw, and we were beginning to realize what we were up against.

Our convoy was made up of fourteen transports and one battleship. We went aboard the transports and anchored for the night in the Hudson River off the harbor. The following day, May 2nd, we left New York and everything that was dearest to us. We watched the Statue of Liberty until an unfriendly fog hid her from our view. Leaving the old U.S. of A. behind, we had to make the best of the situation. We were on an English boat, the Messonabee.[1] The crew treated us with consideration, but our food was not what we were used to. We had bread only once a day. According to English regulations bread and potatoes cannot be on the table at the same time. We had plenty of fish and meat, but the way it was cooked did not make it very palatable.

There were about five thousand men on the boat, and the most it had ever carried before was twenty two hundred and even then it was loaded over capacity. It is easily seen that we were overcrowded. Every conceivable place had to be made use of for sleeping places for the men. In the large mess halls, hammocks were hung in the ceiling so close that they touched each other. The poor unfortunates who slept in them had to get up at four o'clock in the morning as they began setting the tables at that time. The tables, of course, were also slept on.

Although there were several large mess halls with more than twenty large tables in each, it required four sittings to feed the soldiers, and the ones who had the poorest sleeping quarters ate first. I was lucky enough to draw a stateroom that I shared with another boy, and my card said that I was entitled to eat at the fourth sitting. We were so crowded that when we were all on deck we barely had room to stand up. Most of the time some soldiers would be below decks and that gave us more room.

We soon settled down to a daily routine. In the mornings we had physical exercises; in the afternoons we had races and contests, music by the band, and life boat drills. A group of men and an officer were assigned to each life boat. The main object of the drill was to teach us to find our places quickly and without confusion. We were about fifty in our boat and my number was 18. We wore our life belts constantly night and day. To be caught without a life belt meant heavy punishment which no one cared to risk. No lights were allowed after dark that could be seen from the outside, but below decks we had plenty of light. We had fair weather considering the season. At times the ship rocked badly and quite an epidemic of seasickness broke out, but the only time we had high seas was when we were a few days off the English coast.

On account of the German submarines we went north of Ireland, but failed to see any signs of the pirates. It was reported that one of the boats sighted and fired on a submarine, but I don't know if such was the case. When we neared the danger zone we were met by a flotilla of submarine chasers. There might have been six or a dozen, they went by so fast that one could hardly count them. They reminded me very much of a fly or a bee keeping up with your automobile and at the same time making quick excursions to either side, seemingly without effort. They were very small and incredibly fast, and could make sharp turns at full speed like no other kind of boat could. They were armed with small guns and I began to see why the submarines were not sinking any army transports. No submarine could have come near enough to do any harm with these speedy little wasps patrolling every foot of the ocean for miles around. They certainly kept the enemy away from us.

The 16th of May we landed in Liverpool, England and were taken to the railroad station in ferries. Part of the distance we had to walk and we must have been a sight loaded down with our packs and heavy barracks bags until we resembled camels more than human beings. I passed one doughboy who lay flat on his back where he had stumbled over a rail, begging for somebody to help him to his feet as the heavy pack made it impossible for him to get up without assistance.

Arriving at the train station, we were placed eight to a compartment in the small English passenger cars and we thought we were subjected to great inconveniences, but we would live to see the day when we realized that this was luxury and comfort. These were third class passenger cars and quite clean. The ridiculously small engine seemed to have an unknown source of power as we sped along through the country and we were very impressed by the beauty of it. When we left New York everything was dead and frozen, no green grass or grain, no leaves on the trees; here we found almost a different nature. The leaves on the trees were fully grown, the grass and grain of the fertile fields stood fully a foot tall, flowers grew in abundance, and altogether it made us glad to be in England.

I was personally much impressed by the beauty of the country. I cannot find words to express how it affected me. It was a quiet, dignified beauty, which perhaps has helped make the character of the Britisher what it is. The whole country is one huge garden, with well-trimmed hedges separating one man's garden or orchard from his neighbor's. One of the peculiarities of England, and the first that draws your attention, is the total absence of wooden structures. Everything is built of red brick, and they appear to have only one style of architecture, one house seemingly exactly like the other. We passed through very large cities and saw rows of houses, several miles long, every house looking exactly alike. We used to say that if you have seen one house in England you have seen them all.

We went through the university city of Oxford, Birmingham, and other large cities. One of the boys in our car, an Englishman, now a soldier in the American army, was born in Birmingham, and he said that from his seat in the car he could see the house where he was born. It was almost ten years since he left home, but much as he would have liked to, it was of course impossible for him to visit the place of his birth.

Another of England's peculiarities is the neatness and scrupulous cleanliness of everything. Everything was cared for, and even the few wild trees we saw growing were pruned and trimmed just as carefully as if they were raised in a garden. The English people were very kind to us and seemed glad to have us come, but more than three years of a grueling war that drained them of their best manhood and daily took a toll of lives of their sons on the battlefields in France and Belgium had left its stamp on them. They did not have the fiery enthusiasm of the Yankees, who came so fresh, so eager for the fray. They had settled down to a sort of grim determination to stick it out, and went about their daily tasks with a calm that made us wonder. Everywhere young women and girls had replaced men. Even heavy work such as handling of freight was done by women, and not a word of discontent could be heard. It would have taught some of our American Bolsheviks some very useful lessons if they could have watched the English people keeping the home fires burning.

We met several trainloads of wounded English soldiers from the front. These were the first wounded we saw and I noticed some of our boys looked a bit more sober than usual. The wounded, however, were in excellent spirits, and had reason to be, as they were back in their own country, which after all means so much. We also passed long trainloads of tanks: large, new tanks going to the battlefront in France. As we drew closer to the scene of combat we saw more evidence of the war in the shape of guns, cannons, and wagons brought back to England for repairs.

After arriving in Winchester the following night we marched out to a camp three or four miles from the city. We stayed there the following day and the second day we marched to Southampton, where the boat taking us across the English Channel awaited. While waiting in the harbor, we looked over the many different ships docked there. There was a large dry dock where the Olympic[2] rested dry, showing her huge bulk, one hundred feet of which is below the waterline.

Crossing the English Channel

We had a very light breakfast early in the morning before we left Winchester, no dinner at all, and whatever prospects we might have had for supper faded when we got aboard the ship. If we found it crowded on the Messonabee, there was no name for the conditions on this boat. Wherever we happened to stop after boarding, there we stayed, as there was absolutely no room to move about. The open space between the railing and the upper deck was covered by heavy canvas, preventing any view of the sea. After dark we stole away, gliding silently out of the harbor to begin the race with the submarines across the channel. I was shoved behind some kind of machinery on the deck, and after awhile managed to lie down and tried to sleep, which of course was an impossibility. The water running over the deck did not particularly disturb me, but the crowded conditions and the great number of men who stepped on me kept me awake all night.

Le Havre

Early in the morning, May 19th, we landed at Le Havre, France. For an hour or so, after the canvas covering the deck was raised, we had a splendid view of the city. From the harbor the city appeared to it's advantage, and we noticed with curiosity the different style of architecture. We disembarked without any breakfast. They started to serve bread and coffee, but owing to the limited time and the great number of soldiers, not half of us were lucky enough to get even a cup. We marched through the city of Le Havre, enthusiastically welcomed by the population. We continued marching with our heavy packs and wearing our overcoats, although it was very hot, to an English camp several miles from Le Havre. The camp was located at the top of a small mountain so it was an uphill grade every foot of the way and we marched at a very brisk gait. This was the closest I ever came to falling out of formation, and by noon the men were falling out by squads, utterly exhausted.

We had eaten nothing for twenty four hours and were marching in uncomfortably warm weather with packs that were afterwards weighed and found to be between 95 to 105 pounds. When we finally halted at camp, our first task was to get our shoes off and attend to our feet that had sorely suffered from this strenuous hike. In the afternoon we were given a light meal, the first in more than thirty hours. If we expected to get a rest now, we were mistaken. Ordered to fall in, we marched to a camp several miles away to be equipped with gas masks, get our first lesson on how to put them on, and to take our first gas test. We had to march all the way to this camp and back at attention as punishment for the fatigued soldiers falling out on our march earlier in the day.

Incheville

Every soldier must be able to put his gas mask on in six seconds, which the English instructor took great pains to make clear to us. After a struggle of about five minutes most of us finally had our masks on, and I confess I doubted if I ever would be able to put it on within the six second limit. I did, however, become quite proficient in the gas mask maneuver later on. We were next put to the test by going into huts filled with poison gas and staying in there for five minutes. I guess we were all a little nervous but we all made good. We then returned to camp and spent a few days there, during which time we turned in our extra equipment such as heavy underwear, shoes, etcetera.

When we left this camp we marched to a place several miles away where we boarded a train, or rather we were packed into cattle cars, labeled 'Hommes 40 Chevaux 8.'[3] Little attention was paid to 'Hommes 40' as we must have been at least fifty in the miserably small cars. Twenty-five men would hardly have room enough, and trying to sleep was of course out of the question. We left in the evening and once during the night the train stopped and we were served hot coffee. A cup of coffee does not go very far with a hungry man but it is a long ways better than nothing at all, and we were starving as usual.

In the morning we unloaded and began marching to an English camp some miles away. A Scottish bagpipe band met us at the train and preceded us on the march to the camp. They played all the way and as they were dressed in the original native costumes of the Scots, with their saucy caps and kilts showing their bare knees, it was rather a novel experience to be marching to their music. The drummers wore a tiger skin slung over their shoulder and one of them was a past master in the art of handling drumsticks. He kept the sticks up in the air most of the time, all the while keeping step and time and never missing a beat on the drum. Upon reaching the camp we had chow and continued our march until we reached Incheville. This was about the first of June.

My squad was temporarily billeted with a French family and was given the upper story which was better than sleeping outdoors, but the sanitary conditions were such that we eventually moved out of there. The people in the house seemed pleased to have us there and treated us well. We became good friends of the children, a boy and a girl.

We came to Incheville at the time when it looked like the Germans were going to break through to the coast. They captured Amiens and were desperately trying to smash the British line. Abbeville was their immediate objective and since the situation was serious we hurried there to be in reserve in case the Germans should succeed. Incheville is only a few miles south and west of Abbeville, almost on a straight line from Amiens to Treport on the coast.

We heard the big guns booming all the time as the Germans continued their terrific drives, but the British line held, and we were not called on to go to the front. The 33rd Division that came across with us, however, went to the front and took part in many desperate battles. We were drilled as only men who shortly expect to go into the fiercest kind of warfare can be drilled. Under the English drill masters and instructors we went through actual gas tests, besides the daily gas mask drill, bomb and hand grenade throwing, rifle and rifle grenade practice. We sweated and we worked and we were just as anxious to learn as they were to teach us. They told us we improved fast. One of the English soldiers congratulated us on the fact that we were the first group of Americans he instructed in bomb throwing that had no casualties. The Americans were known to be rather careless when handling high explosives.

Like every other place in France they had a prison camp in Incheville and we got so used to seeing German war prisoners that they ceased to be a curiosity, although at first it interested us very much to watch them. When we traveled on the trains they used to wave their hands at us and seemed to be very content to be prisoners. A few shook their fists at us which might have been their way of joking. Incheville is not a very pretty place. The surrounding country was gently rolling and seemed to be good farming land. Small grain seemed to be the principal crop. A large bottle factory was located here which employed a great number of men and women. We used to watch them blow the red hot glass into differently shaped bottles.

We staged sham battles in the woods near the village. One time our platoon was annihilated by the enemy and we were roundly scolded by our commander who said our defeat was due to poor scouting. We had calls to arms at night several times. This call is always unwelcome, but more so at night. We would rush out and march several miles, sometimes double timing up a steep hill with full packs until we thought we could go no farther, then go through a stiff drill before turning back to our billets.

Our rations were very scanty which might have been because we were under British command and had to eat British rations. Around the 16th of June we received orders to turn in the English rifles issued to us, and in true army style we got this order in the middle of the night. It had to be executed immediately, so in pitch black darkness we marched to the supply base and turned in our rifles and ammunition, after which we returned to our billets and turned in. When we left New York we were issued Springfield rifles; when we arrived in France we had to turn those in and were given the English Enfield, which in turn now had to be turned in as we were going to an American sector.

The following morning we left Incheville and began a march which broke all previous records. We made better than sixty miles in less than four days and finished the march with a high average, our battalion ranking highest. We were inspected by General Wright[4] who complimented our major upon our good condition. We camped wherever we happened to stop for the night. Sometimes we slept in old barns and sometimes we pitched our tents. One day a call to arms was sounded while we were bathing in the Somme River, and it sure made us hustle to get into our gear!

3 JOURNEY TO THE FRONT

On The Train From Incheville to Uriménil

When we reached the place we were to entrain, we were issued the American Eddystone[5] rifles and proceeded to load our entire stock of supplies onto the train, and the soldiers were packed into small cattle cars. We were very uncomfortable but tried to make the best of it and made use of the opportunity to study the French people and the country through which we traveled.

France is in many ways much different from the United States. The first thing we noticed were the wooden shoes that everybody, especially in the country, wears. Small babies, children and old people wear them. We saw children skip rope and they apparently had not the slightest trouble in keeping their big wooden shoes on. There are different styles in wooden shoes, as in other shoes. They have a coarse, heavy work shoe and also a finer, lighter dress shoe which is covered by fancy engravings and is oiled. Next we noticed the heavy two-wheeled carts, with wheels that stand six feet high and look very heavy and clumsy. We hardly ever saw wagons with four wheels. They use horses, mules, or even cows to pull their carts. If more than one animal is used they are not hitched abreast but one behind the other. We often saw three horses hitched in this fashion pulling a cart.

Along almost every creek we saw women washing, using a club to pound the dirt out of the clothes. They depend almost entirely on cold water to wash in. All the houses were built of stone with walls almost three feet thick, the outside plastered white. One building served as a combination house, barn, chicken coop, and pig pen, with the manure piled in front of the door on the street, the size of which indicated the health of the owner's bank account.

When we first landed in France we slept in the open. This practice had to be discontinued, however, as the large, fat, French snails disturbed our sleep by constantly crawling over us. These pesky things would come out after sundown to crawl up on our faces, which seemed to be their favorite playgrounds. They left a path of nasty, slimy goo wherever they crawled, and in the mornings we had bright, shiny stripes all over our faces and clothes, showing the routes of the many and different snails that called on us during the night. They were up to three inches long and about one inch thick and mostly black in color, and it was claimed that the French people ate them.

We passed through the outskirts of Paris but as we were not allowed to leave the cars we did not see much of the city. Our train stopped near the American railroad yard and we saw hundreds of large American engines which were like giants compared to the small French and English engines. We saw the Eiffel Tower several hours before we arrived in Paris. It is a very imposing sight and it is so tall that it looks like the top is in the clouds.

The countryside was gently rolling with a few hills covered in a growth of trees. The soil looked like it could produce good crops of grain. Orchards and gardens, however, looked very neglected, which of course was due to the lack of men to take care of them. This absence of men was noticed everywhere. A few old men could be seen here and there, but nowhere were young or able bodied men to be seen, not even boys over ten years of age. What they were doing or where they were, I don't know, unless they were employed in shops or factories. Women were seen in the fields, plowing with walking plows and oxen. Sometimes a horse and an ox would be hitched to a single plow. Sometimes we saw cows pulling heavy loads. Our chief amusement when traveling on the train was throwing pennies to the children who came down to the railroad to see us; watching them scramble to get the pennies was a source of great fun.

We were so crowded in the cars that we hardly had room to lie down. If someone was unlucky enough to have to get up after we had managed to lie down in some manner for the night, he had to remain standing up for the rest of the night as it was impossible to find the place a fellow had occupied.

Our rations consisted of hard tack and corn willy,[6] and once during the trip we had coffee. For three days and nights we traveled thusly and before the journey was over it began to tell on us. Some of us were outright sick and none of us were feeling any too well. Our destination was Uriménil, Alsace, and as we neared the Vosges mountains the country became more wild in appearance, yet it was nearly all cultivated and good crops were growing on the fields. We arrived in the evening about the 15th of June, then unloaded and marched to Uriménil where we arrived late in the night. Assigned to our billets, we soon rested from our tiresome journey.

Uriménil

The main attractions of Uriménil are nil. It is a little inland town about 12 km south of Épinal in the foothills of the Vosges mountains. We drilled here very intensively, and made use of almost every minute. The weather was very good and the few days we could not drill outdoors were spent in lectures and gas mask drills.

We were billeted in an old factory which puzzled us for a long time. We could not make out what they manufactured and could not ask the men around there on account of our limited knowledge of the French language. One day, however, they started the machinery and we discovered that they were making potato flour. It was a large two-story building and true to French style the factory, living rooms, cow and horse barns were all in the same building. The hillsides were all torn up by trenches. Some said they were left from the Franco-Prussian war of 1871, others said they were constructed at the outbreak of the war in 1914. These trenches were of great value to us in training and we pulled off many a stiff battle in them. Sometimes we would defend them and sometimes we would attack and capture the other side.

While in Uriménil we drilled mostly in the woods on a hillside as we had no other drill field other than the road. The drilling was very hard work in itself and when practiced on a steep slope it made it much harder. The people here were poor and seemed to have a hard time making their living. As in all other places in France men were scarce, the women doing all the work. As far as could be seen this was cattle country and they did not raise anything but hay. The fields were really swamps and so soft they would not carry a horse or a load. Consequently every straw that grew on the fields had to be carried by the women on some appliance that looked like a stretcher to the house where they stored the hay. No hay was stacked outside.

At one time the weather looked threatening and our officers called for volunteers to help the people harvest the hay the following day. The next day was Sunday and we were sorely in need of a rest, but a number of us did volunteer. Great was our joy when we awoke the next morning to discover that it was raining, which meant a day of rest for us after all.

We made several trips to the rifle range. This was about seven miles from the place where we were billeted and it was a good long hike. The practice was good for us and we soon became proficient at hitting the targets. Lieutenant Seamon was made second in command of the company and Lieutenant Woodworth was placed in charge of our platoon. He was a good drill master and we liked him very much. At this place we saw the first German aeroplane fly over us. The anti-aircraft guns promptly opened up fire on him and it was reported that they brought him down.

We received orders to leave Uriménil about the first of July. We were roused out of our more or less comfortable beds at 4:30 AM to eat breakfast right away. Our breakfast proved to be none, however, as the cooks were sleepy and let all the rice burn. We each got a small cup of coffee and a thin slice of bread, which we were told was for breakfast and dinner both. About the only way we could work that was to drink the coffee and save the bread for dinner, which most of us did. The ones who ate their bread had to pay for it later in the day. We then went to work and loaded a lot of equipment, supplies, and ourselves into large American trucks and proceeded towards the front. The hills grew higher and the grades steeper as we wound our way through the Vosges Mountains, arriving in Fellering at four o'clock in the afternoon.

Fellering

In Fellering we were unloaded and shown our billets. My squad was assigned to a barn in a parsonage. According to European style the barn was really a part of the parsonage. An old, nice couple, apparently caretakers, a few servants, and two priests occupied the parsonage and seemed glad to have us there.

Fellering is a little town of about 600 population. It is located about 10 km over the German border. This territory was taken in 1914 when the French drove the Germans back about 18 km over the border, the Germans being unable to wrest it back from the French. The people spoke both French and German and we Americans soon were in conversation with them, especially the children, as a large percentage of us spoke German more or less fluently.

The people were quite Germanized and all the men of military age were serving, with or against their will, in the German army, and I think there were many German sympathizers there. I met a man who lived in Philadelphia for 17 years and spoke good English. I asked him if the people here were loyal to France, and he said that all the older people did not ask for anything better than to be French, but some of the younger generation that had grown up under German rule did not care much one way or the other.

We were the first American soldiers in Fellering and they treated us royally. Conditions were vastly different compared to what we observed in other places in France. We could buy chocolate, tobacco, and bread here, things we were unable to procure in other places. Oatmeal, real American Quaker Oats, was another thing we could get here so we bought some and had the old lady of the parsonage cook them for us, which she was glad to do. A large number of the people spoke English and as a whole they looked like a higher class, being better educated than the common people and dressed as only the rich could afford.

With the exception of the Fourth of July, we were busy drilling every day. In the Vosges, high mountains surrounded us on all sides. We had sham battles, attacking large hills and capturing them against heavy fire from the enemy, and won our officers' praise. Owing to the fact that the Germans considered the people in this territory their own, they never shelled this area, and the American officers took advantage of this and drilled us in the open sometimes. This was quite difficult, however, as the enemy planes watched us closely and tried to bomb us whenever they could. One plane dropped two bombs on us one day. One bomb dropped near a factory quite close to us. The other failed to explode. It went down into the ground near our billets, leaving a hole like a badger. We had the satisfaction of seeing this plane brought down by the anti-aircraft guns and watched it fall to the earth, slowly revolving like a wheel. We heard that the pilot was killed but the observer was still living when found.

The Fourth in Fellering

The Fourth of July, 1918 found us in Fellering, and as that day was proclaimed a legal holiday by the French government, both the French and we Americans went to work to celebrate the day. Our regiment had a program consisting mostly of games, races, and band music. We began celebrating by eating the first square meal we had since we landed in France. Our company had a large expense fund and the Mess Sergeant spent it all for food.

Prior to the holiday we received orders to hold ourselves in readiness to go to the front on a moment's notice, to take over a sector of the frontline trenches. This did not interfere with our celebration; we went right on and the program was carried out as originally planned.

In the afternoon of the Fourth, we assembled on the drill field for the main events. There were good horsemen among the American officers, and the French, who have a well-known reputation for being good riders, challenged them. The races were very spirited and a keen rivalry existed between the two nationalities. The honors were even, with perhaps a shade of an advantage going to the French. One of our lieutenants was a former cowboy and crowded the French riders hard. The contestants were all good natured and the races were much enjoyed by all.

We had half and one mile running races between the American soldiers. We had former champions in our bunch and some very good records were made, but on account of the heavy hobnail boots, perhaps no world records were made. A distance jumping contest was also held which was closely watched. My corporal won highest honors in this event.

In the meantime a baseball game had been going on in a corner of the field and was liberally patronized. The French found little interest in this game so it was almost an all American crowd watching it. For some reason the Boche[7] planes were not in any way interfering with our program and we could devote all our attention to the sports and celebration in general.

After the races we had a show and entertainment in the town, given by some of the soldiers from our regiment. Afterwards we had speeches by Major Botger and Captain Thompson of M Company. Captain Sodemann of L Company made a speech in German thanking the people of Fellering on behalf of the American soldiers for the splendid treatment accorded them. In the evening our regimental band gave a concert. This was followed by a moving picture show furnished by the people of Fellering free of charge. In all we had a very enjoyable day and it was appreciated by the French just as much as by us. The French certainly patronized our program. The drill field was crowded with French soldiers and civilians.

4 THE FRONT LINES

A few days previous, Lieutenant Seamon and Sergeant Unrue went to the front line to locate our positions and find dugouts for us. They were gone a few days and when they returned they reported that while they had a pretty stiff scrap while they were there, they felt confident that we would be able to take care of ourselves. We made preparations to leave for the front line. The time that we so long expected had come; we were actually taking our places at the front.

At two o'clock in the morning of July 7th we were called out, and once in formation we began the march to the front. There was a large mountain separating us from the front line trenches. As the crow flies it was perhaps only a couple of kilometers, but the only way we could get there was to follow the road which wound itself around the sides of the mountain, making the distance about 14 km. We marched all night and at eight o'clock in the morning halted on top of the mountain where we camped for the day. We were too close to the Germans to march in daylight.

We climbed the mountain, all the time going higher with every step. If we thought the mountains around Fellering were high, they were as nothing compared to what we had to climb now. These were really the highest mountains of the Vosges, part of the Alps, and we could see the Alps in Switzerland from where we were, about 35 miles away. On account of the mountainside being so steep we had trouble laying down and keeping in place as we were continually sliding or rolling down. In fact, in the evening when we fell in to resume our march one of the boys fell down and broke his leg.

The weather was ideal for moving troops, raining and very foggy, so we started off before it got dark. On top of the mountain marching was easy for a few hours. We passed a graveyard where the Americans who were killed in this sector were buried. There were already a great number of little black crosses, each cross marking the final resting place of a soldier, and as we passed it, silently, these lines written by Colonel John McCrae[8] of the Canadian army came to my mind:

In Flanders Fields

In Flanders fields the poppies blow
Between the crosses, row on row,
That mark our place; and in the sky
The larks, still bravely singing, fly
Scarce heard amid the guns below.

We are the Dead. Short days ago
We lived, felt dawn, saw sunset glow,
Loved and were loved, and now we lie
In Flanders fields.

Take up our quarrel with the foe:
To you from failing hands we throw
The torch; be yours to hold it high.
If ye break faith with us who die
We shall not sleep, though poppies grow
In Flanders fields.

When we reached the other side of the mountain we discovered it not much easier to get down than to get up. Nearing the trenches, we had to be very cautious as the slightest noise would cause the Germans to send up flares, and in the bright light of the flares anything that moved could be easily seen. As soon as a flare went up we stopped dead in whatever position we happened to be in and remained so until the flare died out. It was so dark that we had to hold on to each other, the first man following close to the guide who knew the road. We arrived to our dugouts without any accidents.

The men we relieved told us that as they had made a raid on the Germans a few days before, we should be very watchful since they always tried to even things up and they would be sure to pull off something. I was lucky, or unlucky, I don't know which, to be assigned to day guard duty. Lucky because night guard in the trenches is a terrible strain on the nerves and the weariest of all duties. Unlucky, because we were on duty sixteen hours to the night guard's eight, and besides, the night reliefs and the runners always managed to make enough noise to keep us from getting much sleep. On being shown our sleeping place (mine and Snyder's was the table), the night guards were posted and the rest of us settled in.

Hartmannswillerkopf

Directly in front of us roughly half a mile away was the German town of Hartmannswiller,[9] now nothing but a heap of ruins, part of No Man's Land. Our first lieutenant's name was Hartmann. His father was born in Germany and it is claimed that this town was named after the lieutenant's grandfather. Lieutenant Hartmann used to boast that some day he would lead his men across No Man's Land and capture the birth place of his forefathers. We never learned if he carried out his threat. The line here was held by G.C.'s (Guard Command, French). Ours was G.C. #6, held by about twenty men under the command of Lieutenant Gilchrist and Sergeant West.

I slept fairly good that first night as it was very quiet with only the occasional booming of the guns and a few rifle shots. At nine o'clock in the morning I went into the front line trenches for the first time and was assigned to my post. It was with a feeling of expectancy and something that amounted to happiness that possessed me as I took charge of my post. It was the greatest moment of my life.

I peered cautiously over the top of the trench, expecting to see the Boche, and was very much disappointed not to see any. At our post there were not more than a hundred feet between us and the German trenches, but as the Germans were not any more anxious to be seen by us than we were to be seen by them, we did not see much of each other.

The daily program was something like this. We were in the trenches for the first time and were very eager to get a shot at the Boche. We were there to fight and fight we should. We scanned the enemy positions every minute, and as soon as we thought we saw something suspicious we fired our rifles. When we kept this up for awhile the Boche would get sore and open up on us. The snipers generally started it, followed by their machine guns. To get even we started our machine guns and for good measure sent over a few rifle grenades. This caused the Boche to lose his temper entirely and he would turn his minenwerfers[10] on us. Minenwerfers are quite dangerous as they have a large killing radius, and we had to signal our trench mortar batteries, located behind us, to silence the enemy. We always had the satisfaction of the last word; when things got too hot for us our trench mortars would help us out. We were the first to begin and the last to give up the argument.

This occurred every day, with a few exceptions. At half past three in the morning every man in the trenches stands at his post. This is the rule on every front, French, British and American. The term 'stand to' was borrowed from the English. This is absolutely necessary as the Germans always attack between the hours of three and dawn, and we always had to be ready for them. We stood with bayonets fixed and our eyes on the enemy lines until daylight, when those who were not on duty were allowed to go to their billets. There were some days when there were extra numbers on the program. The second night the Germans attacked us at half past three, like usual, just as we were getting out for 'stand to', in fact the bombardment woke me up. They sent over a terrific shellfire on our trenches, and very soon our batteries were replying, and then every rifle and machine gun on both sides was firing.

It was a terrible strain to stand on the posts, shells whistling past, exploding, and the horrible screams we came to dread so much all around us. The loud explosions made talking out of the question but nobody had anything to say anyway. I and two others were detached to a post in a hole on our left, guarded only in case of attack, with orders not to fire unless we saw the enemy approaching. We stood there, gripping our rifles tightly, bayonets fixed, every muscle tense, waiting for the Germans to come. We were ready.

They did not come this far, however. The attack was directed mainly on the lines held by L and K companies. We were to the left of K company and consequently got our share of the shells but had only four casualties, all wounded but one died later in the hospital. L company, who bore the brunt of the attack, suffered sixty casualties with ten killed. One of them, Joe Pirkl from North Dakota,[11] had his head severed from his body by a large shell. Such high explosives and large caliber shells were used by the Germans in their attack on us that the bodies of some that were hit by shells were never found. In other cases they had to pick up the pieces and carry them away in shelter halves. A load of these wrecked human bodies was carried past the Colonel's headquarters. When the Colonel saw the men he asked what they carried. On being shown the contents, he wept.

K company had about ten casualties so our company came out of it very cheaply. We learned afterwards that the Germans had been reinforced by 700 hand-picked shock troops and came over the top *en masse*. Our artillery fire, together with the machine guns, made it impossible for the enemy to advance and he gave it up as a bad idea after reaching our barbed wire entanglements.

This was a very severe test for us, being only one day old in the trenches. We received our baptism of fire and stood the test. This was acknowledged by both the American and French officials. Not one soldier had flinched even at the moment when it looked like we all would be wiped out. At another G.C., however, one of the sergeants lost his head and was afterwards reduced to the rank of private. The same was said of a lieutenant in anther company.

The following day we were satisfied to leave good enough alone and there was very little firing. One day later we had another mixup. We used to bring the chow to the entrance of a trench, which must have been seen by the Germans, and one day they decided to give us a little surprise. We were standing in line waiting to be fed when Whizz---Bang!, a minenwerfer shell landed in the midst of us, wounding no one but totally ruining the large can we carried our grub in. This breaking up of our dinner party made us real sore but we could do nothing except scatter along the trench as quickly as possible. They sent over a bombardment which lasted several minutes.

Life in the Frontline Trenches

The guns on both sides fired almost constantly. We Americans were more generous in the use of shells, but what the Germans lacked in numbers they made up for in accuracy. Their perfect range was wonderful. Frequently they dropped shells right in our trenches, which is quite a feat when fired at a distance of ten miles.

One day we were subjected to a severe strafing by the Germans. It was around supper time when they opened the bombardment. To show his accurate aim the Boche put some shells at every post, most of the shells landing directly in the trenches. I was by this time on duty at my post and I could see the shells exploding. Quite a number of shells landed around our eating place, then one landed directly on Snyder's post. His post was only a few feet away from mine, and when I heard the incoming shell I crouched down close to the wall of the trench for protection. The force of the concussion when the shell exploded knocked me flat on my stomach. When I recovered from the shock I turned around, expecting to see a dead man, but Snyder was too quick for the Boche. When he heard the shell come he made one big jump for a little dugout near his post and was peeping out through an opening, laughing at me.

Having visited his post, I knew I was next and crouching low once more I awaited the shells. My post had a piece of tin laid across the top of the trench, and in back of me was a large tree. Close to the tree was a German six inch shell that failed to explode when it landed, but remained a constant source of danger. If another shell happened to explode near it, it might cause the dud shell to explode. I did not have to wait long, my shell came very soon. A deafening explosion, a lot of noise on my tin roof caused by flying dirt and branches, and it was all over, for the time being, anyway. The machine gun position to my right was now being attacked. This post had cost a good many lives, and three men were killed there the day we arrived. We did not guard this post in daytime and it proved to be a wise plan.

A general shelling of the whole area was now going on and I heard my name called. Turning around I saw Lieutenant Gilchrist motioning me to come. I went to him and he said "hurry up and get out of here, the Boche is shelling the stuffing out of us!" I now discovered that I was the only one left. All the other men had been ordered to their dugouts, so I headed there, too.

We sent signals to our trench mortars for assistance, who as usual soon made the Boche shut up. My time of duty was up and upon relief I went back to my billet. We took turns getting the chow. The kitchen was located at the foot of the mountain we were defending and it was so steep that in places we had to go backwards when climbing it, digging our heels into the ground to get safe footing. It was real hard work and although we were comparatively safe from the enemy here, every one of us preferred to stay in the trenches than to go for chow.

At night we sent out patrols to explore enemy locations and the Germans did the same. The scouts did this duty and since it's mostly night work, they had nothing to do in the daytime, making the rest of us rather jealous of them. One time when a scout patrol was traversing No Man's Land, the Germans opened up a terrible bombardment on them. One of the boys got separated from the rest and after a good many narrow escapes he finally made his way back to our position. Thinking that every one of his comrades was killed he reported to the colonel that he was the only one left of the patrol. The Colonel laughed and said "every member of the patrol reported back, and you are the last one to get in."

Blueberries grew in great abundance on the hillsides and although we were warned not to eat them, because they might retain some vapor of poison gas, the temptation was too great. We ate them, *lots* of them. Lieutenant Gilchrist said that if we picked the berries he would tell the cooks to make sauce of them, which we did and enjoyed the sauce very much.

It was very cold up here in the mountains even though it was the middle of July. We were issued long leather vests and we wore them all the time, together with all the other clothes that we had. It was raining a great deal, too, which did not help us very much. A lively bombardment duel continued almost all the time. We could see where our shells exploded when they fell in open spaces not hid by the tall timbers, but I don't know what the targets were. Owing to the rough mountainous country, tramways were largely used for transportation of supplies and they were the chief targets of the Germans. One direct or near hit would put the line out of use for several days. The roads were constantly shelled, especially at night. The regimental headquarters, some miles back, would get its share of shells also. Men were killed or wounded almost every day there.

It was while in the trenches at this place that I received my first letters from home and it surely was a day of great rejoicing. I read them at my post, one eye on the letter, the other on the Germans. We were relieved in the evening of July 20th so in the morning we had a little surprise for the Boche. At an exact time decided on in advance we opened up a terrible rifle fire. Every rifle and machine gun worked to its capacity. We kept this up for half and hour and it didn't amount to anything other than throwing a scare into the Boche, but that was all we intended. This was not a very good thing to do but our spirits were high on account of being relieved and we felt that we must do something to celebrate. Our relief at night was accomplished without any accidents, everything working like a clock, and we pulled out, highly elated at taking our first turn in the front line trenches.

We marched all night to the top of the mountain and camped on the same spot where we stopped on our way to the trenches. Later on, after we slept a while, we woke up in time to see German prisoners being escorted under guard to the rear lines. The 137th Regiment went over the top the night we left and captured them. We knew that something was going on as a heavy bombardment continued for several hours. After roasting the prisoners for being pro-Germans we went back to try and get some more sleep.

Kruth

Late in the afternoon of July 21st our company fell into formation and marched down the mountain, taking the road to Kruth this time, arriving there late at night. Kruth is a little town north of Fellering and like that town it was well supplied with tobacco and such stuff, but it was not nearly as clean and the people looked quite sloppy. While at Kruth we made our acquaintance with the first Y.M.C.A. men we met in France. They tried to serve us the best they could but their supplies were not large enough to accommodate all of us.

We spent a single day, Sunday, at Kruth. There were quite a number of French soldiers there also, and a game of soccer was arranged between the French and Americans. The game was witnessed by a large crowd and was well played, but although the French appeared much speedier they were easily beaten by the Americans. The following day we left Kruth in trucks. To get back to civilization we had to cross the same mountain that we crossed going to the front. The road wound around like a corkscrew, following the mountainside for a distance, then turning to go back the opposite direction some fifty or seventy-five feet higher up. I looked down and saw our train of trucks in five different lines directly below us, one seventy-five feet higher than the next, every other line going in the opposite direction.

Saulxures-sur-Moselotte

In the evening we arrived in Saulxures, about 25 km south of Gérardmer, and were billeted in houses about a mile from town. The river Moselotte ran past our billets and afforded us an opportunity to bathe, a luxury in the A.E.F.[12] While here we received the finishing touches in extending our order of attack. The officers certainly made good use of the time to improve on our drilling.

A woman claiming to be a Belgian refugee lived in a room above where the soldiers were quartered. She showed us marks and scars of bayonets where the German soldiers had wounded her. She said that a soldier tore her baby out of her arms and either killed or tortured it. She had two small boys and treated them very well while sober, but she was drunk most of the time and the boys had to stay away from her as she was very violent and often tried to kill them and herself.

One day she was seen lying on the road drunk. The road ran on top of a very steep hill, and at the foot of the hill was a little creek and a lot of rocks. She rolled around, kicking and screaming, then rolled over the precipice. I was in my billet upstairs and could not see the bottom of the hill but all at once I saw the water in the creek colored red with her blood. She had crushed her head on the rocks. I thought she was dead but some of the doughboys carried her on a litter to the hospital and I heard later that she recovered. One of her boys was adopted by a private in our company.

There were many neat little shops in this town and as we just had our very first payday and consequently had a lot of money, we spent a lot in these shops.

We worked out several regimental problems at Saulxures, one time in a heavy rain so when the Colonel got wet enough he gave the order "about face," and we went home, but we were so wet then that it did not matter much if we went back or not. We had difficulty getting clothes at this place. In fact some of the men looked rather ragged. One day when we were having bayonet drill, General Wright, commander of the 35th Division, came to inspect us. He was not at all pleased with our personal appearance, and upon spying Ed Van, who had a rather large hole in his britches, the General lost his temper and inserting his hand in the hole he ripped Ed's pants open clear down to his shoes. "Now go home", he said, "and lie in bed until you get new clothes." He turned to the captain and major and bawled them out proper for not getting clothes for the men. We soon had a plentiful supply of uniforms.

We were in Saulxures about three or four weeks. Around the 15th of August our division was ordered to the front again. We were loaded onto trucks, and winding our way up and around the steep, high mountains of Alsace we reached Col de la Schlucht in the afternoon. After a short march we came to camp Colette, a French camp erected among the tall pine trees right on the border between France and Germany. We stayed here about three days before we left for our positions at the front. We marched the night of August 18th and in the morning we reached Camp Boquet.

Camp Boquet

In 1914 the French drove the Germans back over the border about 10 km at this place, and the line had not changed much since then. We were about 30 km north of Hartmannswillerkopf, where we held the line before. In the morning we discovered that the wooden shacks we slept in a few hours during the night were riddled with shrapnel until the roof and walls looked like sieves. This was done before we came here but we did not discover it until after daylight. We considered ourselves veterans on account of being in the front lines once before, but we were rather anxious to move into the dugouts after discovering the shrapnel marks.

The front line at this place ran in the shape of a horseshoe with Camp Boquet in the center and different outposts all around. Company headquarters were established at Camp Boquet. We were ordered to an outpost and upon arriving there Lieutenant Seamon told us that he was given maps and ordered to establish an outpost at Geschwing, but upon reaching the place indicated on the map as Geschwing he found it had a different name. Since he felt we were in the correct spot, regardless of it's name, he had us paint a sign proclaiming it Geschwing.

At the Front Again - Geschwing

The large sign ordered by Lieutenant Seamon was placed near our shack where we slept. He gave us strict orders that in case the colonel should happen along and inquire for the name of the outpost we were to tell him Geschwing, and if we had any reason to believe that he doubted our word we were to point to the sign and say "the colonel can see for himself."

Lieutenant Seamon was first of all a soldier. He was very strict and was known all over the division for his discipline, but he was also just and if we did our duty we had nothing to fear from him. There were certain rumors about his serving under Villa in Mexico but nobody vouched for the truth of them. His motto was "I believe in fewer and better Germans." He was later killed in the Battle of the Argonne.[13]

Our duties at outpost Geschwing were the lightest we ever had. Each of us stood guard about three hours a day, the rest of our time we spent as we pleased. We didn't even have to get the chow because half of our platoon, located in another dugout, did that. In return, they were relieved from guard duty. We considered that we got the best of this bargain, as getting the chow was no snap. It was almost a mile to Camp Boquet where the kitchen was and there were long, steep hills to climb to get there. Besides, a fellow never knew when the Boche would tear loose with his shells. We had few casualties at this place.

Geschwing was a pretty little place on a hillside, camouflaged so the enemy aviators never could locate it. There was a wooden shack where half of our platoon slept and a dugout where the other half slept. For some reason this was the only place in France that looked like home to me, and it was with the deepest regrets that I left this place. We had all fervently hoped to be permanently assigned to this sector.

In the valley farther down lie the German town of Sulzeran. A single church steeple still stood, fairly intact, but everything else was in ruins. To the left of our post were the ruins of farm houses, and a large orchard surrounded them. We found gooseberries aplenty, along with currants, plums, and raspberries. There were quite a bunch of apple trees also but the apples were too green to eat so we cooked them for sauce. To pick them we had to be in full view of a large German observation balloon that always was prompt to tip off the German artillery, but we thought that the nice, ripe berries and fruit were well worth taking a risk for and we daily visited the orchard.

About 80 rods down a steep hill was a little creek that we used to wash and clean up, and part of the creek was in plain view of the German observation balloon. We did not as a rule pay much attention to it, so every time we got out where we could be seen, the balloon would signal the artillery and we would be shelled for several minutes. Finally the officers ordered that every man had to wash in a certain place, well hidden from the balloon, and we had no more trouble.

There was a trench running alongside the above mentioned creek where we stood guard night and day. The hill was so steep that we had to pull ourselves up by means of a wire in some places, and going to and from our posts was a job we all dreaded. Some of the company was left at Camp Boquet where they had to build and repair dugouts and they were very jealous of us because we had it so soft.

Some very lively fighting took place while we were at Geschwing, but because our positions were quite far back, the Germans, when they attacked, would encounter our first and second battalions primarily. Several times scouting patrols ran into enemy patrols and these skirmishes always resulted in casualties. The German aeroplanes made regular trips over our positions and peppered our trenches with machine gun bullets. Camp Boquet was shelled quite severely many times and they had many casualties. I was writing a letter home, outside my billet, when the Germans started a bombardment so suddenly that I had to leave everything and run for dear life to a dugout, and it took a long while before I had an opportunity to get back and resume my letter writing.

Around the 25th of August, in the afternoon, we rolled our packs and left this comely little burg of ours and headed towards Gérardmer. For some reason we were relieved in broad daylight, the only time that we had ever moved in daytime at the front. A division of French Chinese Colonial troops relieved us. These troops wear the regular French Army uniform. The road to Gérardmer was mostly down grade but this does not make marching much easier as the cadence is quicker. The Germans shelled us some but it did not amount to much. Part of the road where it was in view of the enemy was of course camouflaged, so we were fairly safe.

5 THE SAINT-MIHIEL DRIVE

Gérardmer

We arrived in Gérardmer late at night after a terrible hike. Lieutenant Gilchrist pulled off his boots and showed us his feet, the bottoms of which were raw and bleeding, and he had not carried a pack while the rest of us carried heavy packs. The following day a goodly number of men went to the hospital for treatment after the harsh march of the previous day. Gérardmer is a pretty town. The population might be around 2,000. It is or was a strong military center with large barracks for soldiers built of stone. Each barrack was five stories high and could easily lodge 5,000 men. We were, of course, assigned to the top floor to get the benefit of climbing the stairs I presume. We planned on drilling there but the French authorities put a stop to it as they had no desire to have their town destroyed by air bombs as the Germans would soon discover troops drilling on an open field.

On my arrival in Gérardmer I was very tired and did not feel well. The following day while we were doing physical exercises, I was seized with a sharp pain through my back and chest and went to the hospital to see the doctor in the afternoon. On my arrival they took my clothes away, made me go to bed, and kept me there until the third day when I persuaded them to let me out. I enjoyed my rest in the hospital very much. I had not slept in a bed since I left home five long months before, and here I had a soft bed and clean white sheets. They gave us daily papers which was a huge treat. I was getting very uneasy because I heard that my division was ordered to Saint-Mihiel to wait in reserve for the American Army in their attack, and I did not want to be left behind so I begged the doctors to let me out, which they finally did.

From Gérardmer to Saint-Mihiel

It was about the 29th of August, and when I reached my company's billet I found that they had pulled stakes and left. This was a disagreeable surprise but upon investigation I found our supply sergeant and a couple of the boys sitting on a pile of packs and blanket rolls, waiting for trucks to load it on. They let me ride in a truck and saved me a long hike which the rest of the boys had to make. We rode to Corcieux where a French military camp is located. This was one of the best camps we had ever been at in France, but the water system was poor, as it was all over the country.

We tried to drill but the Boche aeroplanes were so insistently trying to mix with us that we had to stop, which pleased us very much. We mounted our heavy machine guns in the windows of the barracks, ready to fire on the planes in case the French aviators should not succeed in driving the hostile planes back.

After a few days in Corcieux we were loaded on trains bound for Lunéville. We were as usual loaded into cattle cars, about 50 men in each car. We were so crowded that we could neither sit nor lie down, but sat or laid on each other's arms and legs. The ride lasted all night long. When we arrived in Lunéville, we got off the train and marched through the city to the outskirts where we took a hasty, cold breakfast of corn willy and hardtack.

Lunéville is a good sized city and had once been captured by the Germans. It showed the marks of heavy shelling but the inhabitants still lived there. Breakfast being over, we resumed the march. It rained hard and all day we marched, drenched to the skin, until we came to a little French camp in the neighborhood of Saint-Nicolas. It was a town of perhaps 300 population in peace time, and now it boasted of just one old man and one old priest.

On account of lack of men everything was neglected. Manure was piled up in the streets and the filth and unsanitary conditions made it necessary for our commander to send a detachment of troops to clean up the street before we could make camp. This had been a forced march and we were completely worn out and wet, but the news soon spread of a large plum orchard close by and in no time we were eating plums. It took us about fifteen minutes to clean the orchard, which must have contained twenty or thirty acres. The plums were a very welcome addition to our bill of fare, which had not been what we wished it to be.

At this place we saw the largest number of aeroplanes that we had ever seen arise to go over the enemy lines. Thirty-two aeroplanes rose from the field nearby and sailed away in battle formation. This same squadron went over the German lines almost every day. One day a pitched battle was staged right above us between a French and a German plane. They both crashed to the ground and the major sent a detachment of troops to investigate. They returned to report that a piece of a shell from an anti-aircraft gun had gone through the Boche's gas tank, forcing him to descend. The French plane crowded him too close and he turned his machine gun on him, killing the pilot, and the French plane crashed to the ground. The German made a perfect landing and on regaining the ground cooly asked the nearest man for a match to light his cigarette. On questioning, the German aviator said that he was taking a new plane from the factory to a certain place in Germany, lost his way, and came over the French lines where the anti-aircraft guns opened fire on him.

The civilian population in the neighborhood erected barbed wire entanglements all around this place and in the direction of Lunéville. They worked feverishly every night until daylight, only to resume the work the following night. The great haste in which they worked convinced us that they expected a German offensive towards Lunéville and that they were doing what they could to protect their homes from the invaders. We also heard that the Germans always captured this place every fall to spend the winter here and retreated to the old positions in the spring. The fruit in the orchard that we ravaged was picked by the Germans every year since the beginning of the war. We can vouch for it, though, that the Boche did not get the crop of 1918.

About September 7th we left Saint-Nicolas and all that night marched in a heavy rain. Towards morning we halted at an old château and camped there during the day. At night the march was resumed and we reached Nancy in the morning, where we again stopped during the day. We marched through the whole town and found out, to our satisfaction, that it is a large town. The population is about 35,000 and in some parts it is quite modern. It was badly damaged by German bombardment, and enemy planes flew over the city often, dropping more bombs.

The next night we left Nancy in a regular cloudburst. Our packs got so heavy that we nearly dropped from weariness at times. The following day we camped on a hill near the Moselle river. We were soaking wet and it was very disagreeable to lie in the wet grass, but we had to get all the rest we could in order to stand the strain of the grueling night marches.

Saint-Mihiel

After we left Nancy we marched in the direction of Thiaucourt where we were supposed to be the backup reserve for the troops making the drive at Saint-Mihiel. We arrived at a wood the following day, after another hard night's march, and stayed there in reserve for several days while the drive was going on. At one o'clock in the morning of September 12th, we learned that the French and American artillery, which until then had not been equaled, so completely demolished the German line of defense that our men had little difficulty in driving the Germans back and straightening out the Saint-Mihiel salient.[14]

The attack at Saint-Mihiel was a great success. About 18,000 prisoners were captured along with a huge amount of food and war supplies. The boys talked a long time afterwards about the large warehouses filled with apples that the Germans left behind. At one place they captured cows that were at once subjected to a severe milking by the thirsty doughboys. We were only a short distance back of the lines and the heavy bombardment told us very plainly that something was going on. We camped close to the road leading to the front and the prisoners were marched back on this road past our campgrounds. The German machine gunners and artillery men were found chained to their guns when captured by the Americans.

This significant American victory at Saint-Mihiel paved the way for the big Argonne offensive, which began a few days later. The Americans suffered so few casualties that our division was never used, giving us a much needed rest of which we sure took advantage. We were too close to the front to drill so we only had physical exercises and lectures; outside of that and dodging bombs from hostile planes we had nothing to do. It was raining and we were wet nearly all the time, but we were used to it now.

Privates Dan and Charley decided to stay in Nancy when the rest of us left. They returned one evening after dark, pitched their tent, and lit a candle - which of course was against the rules. The major happened to come along and noticed the light, and after a lot of cussing and argument he got them out of their tent. When he recognized them, he placed them under arrest for lighting the candle and for desertion.

They were not far from my tent when they started arguing again, and soon there was a free-for-all fight. Charley, the boxing champ of the company, knocked the major on his back and gave the captain a few licks as well and it took quite a while to hush the matter up. Courts-martial were held. I did not hear the verdict except that they were sentenced, for one thing, to march with full packs for three hundred hours, outside of drill time. As long as we were at this place we watched them march up and down the road with their packs on, under guard.

6 BATTLE OF THE ARGONNE

About the 18th of September we received our orders to move to the Argonne.[15] In a heavy downpour of rain, we loaded our kitchens and supplies on trucks. After that we rolled our packs and were soon hiking again. For some unaccountable reason the march was done in daytime. We headed towards Domèvre where we boarded French trucks. We passed the main road to Verdun and that road, which is macadamized[16] and about thirty-five feet wide, was crowded with trucks loaded with soldiers and supplies for the front. Four lines of trucks were on the road, two lines going north and two lines going south. In the late afternoon we passed through Toul, a large town, quite picturesque, and strongly fortified.

We were crowded, twenty men in each truck with rifles and big packs, and the conditions in the trucks soon became unbearable. Much as we hated hiking, we gladly would have gotten out and marched. The situation was temporarily relieved when two or three fellows got out and climbed on top of the truck, but the heavy rain drove them back in again. We got along the best we could. We rode all night, passing long columns of French soldiers and trains of supplies and artillery going to the front. We saw heavy artillery including a large number of 14 inch guns plus a countless number of smaller guns. It gave us an inkling that something big was going to be pulled off shortly.

In the morning of September 19th we reached Vaubecourt, where we unloaded. The French drivers never left their seats after we left Domèvre, a run of eighteen hours. Once in a while a driver fell asleep, running his truck into the ditch. We were as tired as they were, but without rest the order to move was given, and we continued to march all day until we reached a woods where we pitched our tents, as usual in a heavy rain. Our dinner of hardtack and coffee was quite a treat as meals, however scanty, were now few and far between.

We laid down to sleep as soon as we had eaten, but we had no more than slid down when the order to fall in was given and the weary march continued all through the night. We camped in the woods near a French camp at Autrecourt. There were barracks here but they were occupied by French troops, and furthermore we were out of the habit of sleeping indoors. We were now as nearly all-in as we ever were, and fervently hoped for a few days' rest. Our hopes were dashed, however, and at eight o'clock in the evening we rolled our packs and headed out for a place north of Clermont[17] where we would hold the second line trenches, one mile back of the front line, until the big Argonne drive began.

It was a beautiful night. The rain ceased, the wind died down, and the full moon shone on the countryside, dotted with figures of men silently moving forward in an endless chain. We halted a brief moment in Clermont while our officers got their instructions from the French guides who met us. Clermont was once a beautiful town, that much could still be seen. Parts of what used to be magnificent residences still remained, but all were damaged beyond repair. The population might have been around 600.

The Germans began shelling us so we moved on in artillery formation, fifty yards between platoons, fifty feet between squads, all in single file. In this formation we continued the march until we reached the place designated to us. It was pitch dark in the woods, the mud was knee deep in places, and all we had to guide us was a small wire strung along the pathway. We were assigned sleeping places. The dugouts were filled first and the rest had to sleep in shacks and tents. Being in the last squad, I and three others were detained to stand guard during the night.

Preparing for the Argonne Drive

When I arrived at my position in the Argonne I was put on guard. I guarded a machine gun post and also acted as gas sentry, and *tout de suite* a Boche plane dove into sight. Flying very low, he riddled my post with machine gun bullets. He kept flying around in a circle and since I had to do the same to keep under cover, he kept me running for dear life around a dugout near my post for quite a while. When I was relieved I tried to get some sleep, but it was so cold that I could not, and soon got up to get warm. We spent a week here, working hard most of the time, carrying supplies and ammunition from the dumps and storehouses.

The Germans shelled this place severely, and in 1914 some very hard fighting took place here. The ground was torn up, with shell holes everywhere, and while we were there they shelled it every day and we suffered several casualties. My squad was in a dugout that formerly sheltered a large French gun, so half of the wall facing the front lines remained open. Our dugout was a twin; that is, there were two dugouts built together. When the shelling was severe we moved way back to where the space turned to one side, forming a tunnel-like opening where we were safer.

One night the Boche was putting his shells so close to our dugout that the corporal told us to get up and retreat to our safe corner. I was the last one to leave and just as I left the part of the dugout where we slept, dirt and branches and rocks descended on me. A shell had hit just outside the opening, and the force of the concussion sent me on my way a little faster than I intended to go. Fortunately I was unhurt and when the bombardment lifted we went to see how our neighbors had fared. In one side of the steel wall was a big gaping hole just above where one of the boys was sleeping. The shell came in at such an angle that if he had been lying in his usual position the shell could not have missed his head. The projectile went through the thick steel wall and several feet into the earth where it exploded, forcing the edges around the hole back like cloth or paper.

The Germans gassed us a lot here. Hardly a night went by that we did not wear our gas masks. The gas sentries were inexperienced and nervous and of course sounded many false alarms. A lot of wild loganberries grew nearby and I made many a meal of them. They were delicious.

According to the map we were right back of Vauquois, which was the right flank of the 1st Army Corps consisting of the 28th, 35th, and 77th divisions with the 92nd in reserve. The left flank rested on Vienne-le-Château. We were about 35 miles northwest of Verdun and about eight miles south of Varennes[18] which was captured by my battalion in the evening of the first day of the Argonne drive; Captain Skinker, the commander of I company being killed in the furious charge. On the evening of September 25th the order came at nine o'clock for us to assemble in front of company headquarters. We knew what it meant and although we were worn out after a hard day's work carrying ammunition, we were eager to move to the front and quickly assembled in the dark.

To the Argonne Front

The night was very dark and everything was quiet. The Boche always used to shell us about that time of the night but he seemed to have forgotten us this night. We were mistaken. We had barely assembled into platoons when we heard the whistling of shells and were subjected to a severe strafing. The order to scatter was quickly given and still more quickly executed. We were lucky enough to escape without any casualties.

Next came a sample of the Boche's uncanny knowledge of the movements on our side of the line. It was the Boche's habit to shell the dugouts and the guns behind us. This evening, however, he did not shell the dugouts as there were no men in them. How he knew that at that particular hour we were in front of company headquarters, I don't know, but the fact is that he dropped the shells right where the company was assembled.

The command came to fall in and after a few minutes we were ready to begin the eventful march to the front. We had just reached the main road when the Boche lifted the barrage that he had been pouring on the company headquarters area, and the road now became his target. All the way to the front he followed us with his shells, his aim and range being nearly perfect, the shells falling, if not in the middle of the road, not very far from it. From the time we left our company headquarters, I noticed a rifle firing in the distance, at intervals from one to five minutes, sometimes one shot and sometimes two or three or four in succession. I am convinced that a German spy was working in the vicinity and was conveying information of our movements to the enemy by means of gunfire.

We reached the first front line trenches, Company I being the only one in our battalion to suffer any casualties from the German shell fire. Turning to our right, we entered a trench which I noticed was kept in very good condition with a wooden board floor and sides reinforced with a netting of willow branches.

If a German officer had been with us he could not have directed the artillery fire better. As soon as we left the road and entered the trenches the shelling of the road ceased, and since we were now in a position where gas would work to the best advantage, the Boche began firing gas shells over low places like shell holes and trenches. The order to put on gas masks was given as soon as the first trace of gas was discovered which was sneeze or tear gas. This gas makes a soldier sneeze and his eyes run, making it impossible for him to keep his mask on. After this gas has accomplished it's mission a deadly gas is sent over to finish off the victim.[19] We all got our masks on in time and the march continued until we reached the dugouts that were to shelter us until the time came to go over the top.

Over The Top

We had no real idea of the big offensive planned here in the Argonne. Up to the last minute we knew only that we were going to attack. Just before we left for the front we were told that Marshal Foch[20] had given the order to attack and that we were to keep on going until the Germans gave up and the war was won. This was exactly the command we had been waiting for and it pleased us highly. We were very anxious to lick the Germans and have this thing over with so we could go home.

The Argonne Forest was considered the hardest area to attack on the whole allied front. French and British military experts agreed that it was impregnable, and the French lost many thousands of men in 1914 and 1915 trying to drive the Germans from these entrenched positions. Several German lines of defense such as the Hindenburg, Siegfried, and Kriemhild lines run so close together here that they constitute a single solid line of defense, manifold stronger than any other part of the Hindenburg line.

General Pershing[21] knew his doughboys, however, and personally asked Marshal Foch that the Argonne be given to the Americans as their sector, and Marshal Foch is said to have answered "Go for it. If the Americans can not advance in that sector, no one can." The Americans tried to keep the Germans ignorant of their presence here by keeping French soldiers in the front line trenches, but it is very doubtful if the Germans were deceived.

In front of us was a large hill. This was to be blown off the face of the earth by our artillery fire, and our company was to advance around it to the right. Another company was to go to the left and we were to join forces on the north side of the hill.

When we went over the top the following was the order from right to left: the 3rd Army Corps from the Meuse to Malancourt, with the 33rd, 80th, and 4th divisions in line and the 3rd division in reserve; The 5th Army Corps from Malancourt to Vauquois with the 90th, 37th, and 91st divisions in line and the 32nd in reserve; the 1st Army Corps from Vauquois to Vienne-le-Château with the 35th, 28th, and 77th divisions in line and the 92nd in reserve. The army reserve consisted of the 1st, 29th, and the 82nd divisions.

In all, the following American divisions were used in the Argonne fight: the 1st, 2nd, 3rd, 4th, 5th, 26th, 28th, 29th, 32nd, 33rd, 35th, 37th, 42nd, 77th, 78th, 79th, 80th, 82nd, 89th, 90th, and 91st. We fought against the Germans who were under the command of the Crown Prince[22] and he used forty-four German divisions in his desperate, but fruitless efforts to stop us.

As soon as we reached the dugouts at the front, but not until the last man was well inside, the Boche ceased his shell-fire, Company A this time losing some men. Our company so far suffered no casualties. It was two o'clock in the morning. Shortly, the bombardment that has never been equaled in volume and magnitude would commence.

We were packed in like sardines in the dugouts. It was damp and soon we were shivering with cold. Our stay in the dugouts was not to be long as was made evident by the order not to remove our packs, and after awhile orders were given to load our pieces and then we heard "everybody out!" We all crawled out and what burst upon our sight and hearing will not be forgotten if we live to be a thousand years old.

Heavy clouds of smoke enveloped everything like a dense fog. We stood for a second, breathless, before this wonderful revelation. Our guns, French, English, and American of every caliber, from the French 75's to the American 14 inch naval guns, lined up in places hub to hub, were strung out behind our lines for sixty miles, every one of them discharging shells as fast as human hands could load them. So heavy was the firing that the flashes from the different guns made a light that looked like a brightly illuminated city when it is approached in a fog.

The whistling of the shells overhead blended into a sort of horrible music that fascinated us but which spelled death and disaster for the enemy. In the deafening roar of the bombardment we could not tell if the Boche was replying with his artillery, but it is very unlikely that he did.

The whole of the 35th Division was now outside the dugouts and the task of assembling into the proper formations began. There was no hurry or confusion. We took our places in rank and soon were at the jumping-off place, in this case the extreme front trench.

The place of honor when going over the top is conceded to the organization selected to go in the first or front wave. Of the twenty-one divisions used in the Argonne drive, nine went over as first wave and amongst them was ours, the 35th Division, and of the regiments the 138th (ours), and of the battalions the 3rd, also ours.

We were assigned to our respective places in the trenches. Captain Thompson, with his staff, remained in the rear of the trench where he stood, watch in hand, every five minutes calling the time. "Boys," he said, "you have thirty minutes before you go over... 25...20...15...10...5 minutes now, 3... All ready, over the top, forward!" The moment had come.

We lively scrambled over the bank of the trench which was about six feet deep. I had the evening before been transferred into an automatic rifle squad as loader and carrier. I was loaded down with ammunition for the rifle and had quite a little trouble getting over. We were soon over, however, and proceeded toward the enemy position in single file, platoon formation, with about sixty feet of distance between each platoon. The zero hour had been set at 5:30 AM and it was still dark. Openings had already been cut in our wire entanglements and we had no trouble getting through.

The Boche threw liquid fire on us but it did not stop us for a second. We advanced at a steady, slow gait and soon crossed the enemy's front line trenches. They were evacuated and we found no Boches there. Dawn appeared, but the fog was so thick that we could not see farther than fifteen feet ahead. We had a most beautiful rolling barrage going, and very nearly suffered casualties from walking into it.

We encountered detachments of enemy troops. On our right all of a sudden we heard a burst of machine gun fire. It happened while we were charging a heap of ruins from an old mill, and our boys, a little too excited, fired towards the sound of the guns, unfortunately wounding several of the men of our first platoon. The fog, of course, was the cause of this. We met the Germans face to face at a bridge across a small stream at nine o'clock. It was only a few minutes work to clear the place, either killing them or taking them prisoner. As was very fitting, Captain Thompson took the first prisoner, a German non-commissioned officer, single handed.

From then on we fought our way through against machine gun fire, mostly, and snipers. The Germans fired until we came close and then they threw up their hands to surrender, crying 'Kamerad'. The dugouts, however, proved to be the richest sources of bounty, every dugout yielding from one lone Boche to sometimes a hundred scowling human hyenas, which were promptly taken care of.

On we went, through miles of barbed wire and brush and rivers until we came to what looked to be a very strong German position. As soon as we were out in the open the captain commanded "on skirmishers", and we quickly extended in a single wave, five paces interval between each man, never slackening the advance. By the time we arrived at the foot of a steep hill, on top of which were the enemy positions, we were so far ahead of the rest of the troops that the captain halted us for a few minutes. As soon as the command to halt was given, we dropped to the ground, exhausted. We saw Germans in large groups on the hilltop and it looked like we were going to meet with stiff resistance.

By our rapid advance we exposed our flanks to the enemy, and we were not here very long before a runner came towards us. He inquired for our captain and all out of breath he reported that a large force of Germans was preparing to attack us in the rear. This was a serious situation, but the captain turned to Lieutenant Hickam and cooly remarked "there you see lieutenant, if we don't keep our eyes open we are liable to get shot in our seats!" Then, turning to his men, he said "boys, this hill is our first objective. We will take it or die in the attempt. Afterwards we will take care of the Germans in our rear. Forward! March!"

The Germans sent across a stiff machine gun fire, but we quickly gained possession of the hill and captured many prisoners. Company L caught up with us and we hastily took up positions to meet the attack in the rear. Some of the troops behind us must have repulsed the Germans, however, as the attack failed to materialize. Information arrived that the Germans were going to counter-attack on the front and we were ordered to dig in. We went to work and soon had a shallow place dug for each squad, then we tried to snatch a few minutes rest. The fog cleared away, the sun shone brightly, and the weather was ideal. The German planes continually flew above us, pouring down a rain of machine gun bullets. We were too tired to pay any attention to them. The Americans must have beat the Boche to the attack; the order for the whole front to advance was given and our dreams of rest were shattered.

7 WOUNDED IN ACTION

We received orders to attack and capture the town of Varennes, located in the valley in front of us. We advanced in the direction of Varennes, our object being to flank it on the north. To Company I later in the evening fell the honor of capturing it. We had for a few minutes been sheltered by trees and bushes, and as we came out in the open the Germans opened a terrific shell fire and we suffered many casualties.

It was around three o'clock when we met the fiercest resistance we had so far experienced. We were advancing slowly in artillery formation, the officers ordering us to get down when the shelling was severe. We stayed in that position until the command to rise was given. The officers ignored their own safety by standing upright, which may have been one of the causes of the heavy casualties among them.

It was at such an occasion that a shell exploded near me, and I felt as if a giant hand had been laid on my shoulder and forced it down. A fragment of a high explosive shell hit me, very likely a six inch shell. I heard the command to rise and go forward, and saw the boys get to their feet to continue the advance. I was left behind, alone.

A very loud groaning beside me, however, convinced me that I was not alone. Struggling to my feet, I saw a boy out of my own platoon trying to walk on one leg. He was wounded in the leg by a piece of the same shell that hit me. Before getting up I managed to unfasten all the straps that held my pack on, in fact I had to do this before I was able to get up, but this fellow had his full pack on plus his rifle. It looked so ridiculous that in spite of my pain I could not keep from laughing, and asked him what he intended to do with his equipment. He could not find any valid reason for carrying the pack and as he was perfectly unable to do so in the first place, I helped him get rid of it.

A Boche sniper turned his machine gun loose on us so we immediately got interested in seeking cover. There were plenty of shell holes and we each found one and crawled into it. That they were half filled with water and we got our feet wet was of no particular concern to us. The sniper kept us in our holes quite a long while, and whenever we tried to get up he would let loose a burst of bullets that came very close at times. Eventually I succeeded in getting up and had gone a few paces, probably exactly what the sniper was waiting for, when a rain of bullets whizzed past me. It was too late to get back to my old hole, so I quickly found another and reached it safely. I was weak and stiff and getting down in the hole took considerable time. The sniper was either a second-rate one, or the distance too great, and the bullets missed me.

After awhile I looked over the edge of my hole and saw that my partner had left his hole and made considerable progress. This meant, of course, that it was all clear so I scrambled out of my hole and since my legs were intact I soon overtook him. He met up with a doughboy who volunteered to help him back to the dressing station, so I passed them and set out on my own. I saw wounded almost everywhere, struggling back to the first aid station. Many were lying on the ground very still, some were dead and others simply too weak or too badly wounded to move or talk. One man had both legs torn off. They were all victims of the barrage the Boche was treating us with.

Our Red Cross men[23] were seen all over the battlefield picking up the wounded and carrying them back to the dressing station. They wear a white band with a red cross on their sleeve, originally intended to show their identity and make them safe from enemy fire as they were caring for the wounded. Every soldier in the world respects this mark, but for the Germans it is a favorite target and they never fail to fire on a man wearing the insignia of the Red Cross. They frequently used red cross marks to mask some fiendish maneuver of theirs. Knowing that the Allied soldiers would not fire on any Red Cross man they would, for instance, send a couple of men with the insignias carrying a load on a stretcher that looked like a wounded soldier towards the Americans' position. Once in place they set it on the ground and, removing the covering, revealed a machine gun that they fired point blank at us, killing a lot of men before our soldiers realized the hideous trick.

I was lucky to find the first aid station nearby. About an hour later I was given first aid treatment at either the 363rd or 364th Regiment's first aid station. The first aid is very simple. Every soldier at all times carries on his belt a small pouch containing a sealed tin box in which is a short roll of medicated bandage. The medic opens the tin box and bandages the wound and then it is all over. No medicines or solutions are used. The station was in a very good location inside a large German dugout that we captured a few hours earlier. It had four different apartments with board floors and it was quite up-to-date. After being dressed we sat around waiting for the ambulances the rest of the afternoon, but none came owing to the congestion of the roads. We finally realized that we had to spend the night so we laid down, those of us who could. A few of us had bunks, but no covering of any kind; others laid on the floor. None of us slept. The groaning and crying of the seriously wounded kept everyone awake. Lying on my bunk, I listened to the conversation of the officers. During the night an officer came in and called the division commander on the telephone. He anxiously asked for reinforcement, saying that he needed both men and ammunition as all their ammunition was gone, and added that if he did not get the reinforcement they would be forced to retreat. I don't know if he got any.

In the morning it soon became clear that we would never get anyplace by waiting for ambulances, so those of us who were able set out afoot to the nearest Red Cross station. I was feeling pretty rotten and had no appetite, but I knew I had to eat something if I were to make it to a hospital. I spied some salmon on a plate in a corner and I grabbed a handful of it, forcing it down with great difficulty. I looked around and found a canteen filled with water. This I took and we started off. We made pretty fair time as we were not completely worn out yet, and the poison in our wounds had not spread and got to working much. Our goal was another Red Cross station farther back of the lines where we heard the ambulances would come. We finally made it but there were no ambulances. They had a fire and were serving hot coffee, tomatoes, and hardtack. They offered me some and I succeeded in drinking some coffee and eating a little of the tomatoes. With the exception of the salmon I had in the morning this was the first I had eaten in thirty-six hours, but my appetite was all gone now.

Many dead bodies were lying on the ground all over the place, both Americans and Germans. It was rather ghastly to sit and try to eat a meal with the corpses so close, close enough almost that I could reach them with my hand. The shells landed around us and every once in awhile we would have to run to an earthen bank nearby for cover. It did not take long for me to decide that I had to get away from this place, which got hotter by the minute.

I was decidedly on the bum now, but anything was better than this Red Cross station where a fellow never knew when he would get bumped off. I started off but made pretty slow progress until a Y.M.C.A.[24] man passed me in an automobile and picked me up. He took me all the way to the next Red Cross station, passing the rest of my company who started out with me from the first station, riding in big army trucks.

Arriving at the station we found them busy loading trucks with wounded, so I just stepped from the car into a truck and was off again.

I watched several German prisoners eat their dinner of American hardtack and corn willy. They were the best-looking Boches that I had ever seen. They were clean and looked rather contented. We rode in the trucks until we came to a place where the road was destroyed, either by the Germans when they retreated or by the heavy shellfire that still continued. We were compelled to get off our truck and I experienced plenty difficulty doing so, my wound increasingly more painful every hour. An infantry captain in the truck behind us scolded the driver severely for making me get off, not knowing that the road was impassable to all.

Ambulances at Last

The Red Cross erected a temporary station nearby and we waited a couple of hours before we learned that owing to the severe fighting at the front and the consequent need for ammunition, nothing except ammunition trucks would be allowed on the roads until further orders. This meant no ambulances for a long time, so we set out on foot once again.

I was filled with misgivings this time. I felt weak, and my wound needed attention. Sure enough, unable to keep up with my company, I was soon trudging all alone down the road. I thought that the traffic on the road was heavy in the morning when I started out, when I met twenty-five tanks merrily rolling towards the front, dodging trucks and wagons and soldiers; but what I saw now was a road where everything from the smallest motorcycles to the largest army trucks and huge naval guns crowded together until it was a solid, surging mass of matériel.

At no time was it possible for me to get on the road. I made the best of it on the side of the road, over shell holes, barbed wire, dead horses and dead men. The shells were falling with a monotonous regularity but did no great damage. A whole division was camping for the night on a hillside on their way to the front. Passing their field kitchen, the boys and the cooks hanging around coaxed me to take supper with them, but a cup of coffee was all I could stand just then. We were on the outskirts of what once had been a city but now it was all in ruins. I knew that another Red Cross station was close and after inquiring directions from the military police I managed to make my way there. The last few rods I had to be assisted by a Red Cross man who came out to meet me.

I awaited the arrival of the ambulances while lying down on a cot of wire netting, and as soon as they arrived we were loaded on them. We were all stretcher cases now and it would be sixty-seven long days until I would be able to walk on my feet again. The hospital we were headed to was not very far, but with the road being used entirely for transportation of war supplies for the front, we had to make a roundabout trip on other roads that made it several miles farther.

I now experienced my first real suffering of the war. The stretcher I was lying on was not properly hung, and every little jar of the ambulance caused it to bump against the wall and the pain me made me cry out loud several times. Our artillery guns were placed all along the road we traveled and kept up a continuous bombardment. We arrived finally at our destination which proved to be sort of a triage center. Those who could be moved were sent farther back of the lines, and the slightly wounded were sent to camp hospitals way back of the lines. I was promptly carried out again and loaded into another ambulance. This time my stretcher was properly adjusted and the trip was made in fine shape, and we arrived at the hospital in the morning of September 28th.

The First Hospitals

I was at once carried into the X-ray room and examined. Owing to the many wounded brought in, they did not have time to take regular photographs but used instead a small X-ray machine that they placed right on the body, moving it around until the foreign objects had been located, marking each place with a black cross so the operating surgeon knew exactly where to cut to find them. This process took only a few minutes and then they carried me into the operating room and put me on the table. It was a large room with fifteen tables, a surgeon and a couple of nurses at each, every one slashing the wounded open and extracting pieces of shrapnel and bullets and amputating arms and legs as fast as they could.

I heard the nurse say "Take another deep breath. That's a boy," and then I do not remember anything until I woke up in a strange bed with nurses and many other things that were unfamiliar to me. It took me the longest time to figure out what had happened to me. With the help of the nurse I finally got things straight, but it was very confusing, with visions of soldiers, Boches, guns, and memories of bursting shells and shrapnel and long painful rides in ambulances, everything getting mixed up in my mind.

I did not know at the time but found out later that this was Field Hospital #145, and I have no clear recollection of my stay. The following day I was put on an American Red Cross train and taken to Base Hospital #42.[25] The American Red Cross trains are very comfortable and they took good care of us. There were many seriously wounded on this train and judging by the way they groaned they must have suffered very much. Base Hospital #42 is located in Bazoilles, near Neufchâteau, not very far from the place where Joan of Arc was born. When we arrived I was taken to ward #14 where they kept the more serious cases. We got along splendidly here and were treated well. Several men died during my stay.

After a couple of weeks or so Major Gamble[26] decided that I had a contagious disease and moved me to the epidemic ward #21. My wound gave me considerable trouble and the doctors, after many consultations, agreed that another operation was necessary so in due time I was carried into the operation room. This time I was saved from the knife by Colonel Harrison,[27] one of the most skilled surgeons in the A.E.F. He said that he thought it would be better to wait awhile and observe further developments. I was carried out again and taken to my old ward #14 where I remained until November 1st.

All this time I was given the best of care by nurses and attendant physicians. It is a fact that the closer a person is to the front line, the better care he gets in the hospitals, and every time we moved some little comfort was dispensed with. November 1st we were transferred from Base Hospital #42 to Camp Hospital #59[28] located at Issoudun about 150 miles south of Paris. We rode on a French passenger train that had been converted into a hospital train. We were carried right into the cars on our stretchers by Algerian soldiers and were hung up by chains fastened from the roof. In the evening of November 2nd we arrived at Issoudun and were soon settled in our respective wards. I was assigned to Ward C on the third floor. We later moved to the top floor.

Issoudun

Issoudun is one of the most ancient of the European cities. It has a population of about 14,000 but is not a very attractive place, as many of the inhabitants are poor and their homes show it. It was founded many hundreds of years ago, and there still remain bridges across the rivers that were constructed before Christ was born. It was destroyed by the Romans under Julius Caesar who afterwards built up a new city on the ruins of the old. He constructed a great stone wall around the city and parts of this wall remain to this day. There are several forts and towers and large buildings left that he erected. One of the streets is still named Avenue de Rome, named by Caesar. The city was destroyed by fire later, but the above mentioned relics remain.

North of Issoudun the Americans built an aviation field, the largest in the world, where they trained their flyers. Major Lufberry, the American ace, and Quentin Roosevelt trained here.[29] An ammunition plant located near the city turned out a large number of shells daily and a lot of German war prisoners were employed there.

The hospital was a large building that, before the war, served as a school for boys studying to become priests. It was five stories high, covered more than a city block, and was built around a courtyard with a very pretty garden in the center. There would have been room easily for 5,000 patients in this building. Parents sent their boys here from every part of France, but now there were only a few students, perhaps a hundred. The building was owned by a rich Frenchman who charged only $35 per month rent to the Americans.

Issoudun was the home of the great writer Balzac. I visited his home, a very pretty château about a mile from the city. Everything remains the same way it was when he lived.

It was at times very lonesome in the hospitals, and very little happened to break the monotony. The most important happening was of course the signing of the Armistice, November 11th, 1918. There was great rejoicing in the hospital and also in the city of Issoudun. Pilots from the aviation field gave exhibitions of fancy flying in the afternoon. They flew directly over the city and hospital and thrilled the people with hair-raising stunts. Many bands were playing, both French and American, and everywhere great joy was manifested that the war was over. Unable to leave my bed, I missed all the celebrations.

A few days later one of the principal streets of Issoudun was rechristened to 'Avenue de President Wilson' in honor of our president. This act was attended by a great parade of school children and townspeople. Many speeches were made in which President Wilson and America were lauded. Singing was a very prominent part of the program and many different bands rendered beautiful selections of music. I missed this also as I could not be out of bed yet.

November 28th was Thanksgiving Day. We heard rumors that we were having turkey and for the whole last week we have not talked about anything other than the big dinner. Sure enough, we had turkey and pumpkin pie and it made such an impression on us that it will never be forgotten by those who were present. In the evening we had entertainment in the mess hall which was greatly enjoyed by everybody, and we all felt that this was the end of a perfect day.

December 2nd was another great day, because on this day I walked out of the hospital for the very first time. I was very weak and after being out for two hours, walking around on the streets, I got very tired and had rather a hard time getting back to the hospital and climbing the four long flights of stairs. I had been in the hospital, in bed most of the time, nearly ten weeks.

December 23rd, the day before Christmas Eve, was cold and rainy and disagreeable all around. The stoves in the hospital smoked very badly and soon the whole ward was filled with smoke. We had a very bad day.

December 24th, Christmas Eve, was a little chilly but it did not rain. Red and I went out in the afternoon to give the town the once over. We found the streets crowded with all kinds of people - French and Yankee soldiers and civilians, all busy doing their Christmas shopping. The small shops had very attractive window displays and certainly knew how to display the wares to their advantage. In the evening a Christmas tree was brought into each ward, the ward was decorated with holly, and this created a real Christmas feeling. After taps had blown the Red Cross girls and some of the boys decorated the tree, then around eleven o'clock Santa Claus with reindeer and bells came in and deposited on each bed a pair of socks filled with nuts, candy, cookies, handkerchiefs, raisins, cigarettes and matches. After this a quartette sang 'Silent Night, Holy Night' and Santa Claus departed. We turned on the lights, strictly against regulations after taps, and staged a celebration that lasted until one o'clock in spite of the night orderly's desperate efforts to make us boys keep quiet.

December 25th, Christmas Day, we woke up bright and early and examined our stockings before breakfast. They carried my meal to me right in the bed so I did not have to get up and dress for breakfast. At eleven o'clock we had religious services in the ward. A chaplain from the aviation base spoke to us, and he surely made us feel like it was Christmas. I shall long remember that sermon. We also had the privilege of listening to several solos by some Y.M.C.A. lady workers and some selections by a quartette.

For dinner we had beaucoup turkey with gravy, dressing, lettuce salad, and currant pie. This was the second time I ate turkey and pie in France and we were beginning to fear that they might spoil us. In the afternoon about twenty-five or thirty negro soldiers put on a show in our ward. Their program consisted mostly of singing and clog dancing. One of the numbers was a negro jigging a most amusing step to the tune of 'Turkey in the Straw' played on a mouth harp by Captain Faucett. In the evening we had another event, a minstrel show put on by some of the boys, the usual jokes being cracked. The entertainment was good and we appreciated it very much. After the show was over, tobacco and cigarettes were distributed, each man getting as many as twenty-five packages. We were getting more tobacco than the demand called for but the surplus was readily accepted by the French, who had difficulty procuring tobacco and were willing to pay or give us almost anything in return for our smokes. A good deal of it was exchanged for wine and liquor.

December 26th the weather was nice. Red and I went out but found everything rather quiet. The town looked almost deserted. Evidently the people were resting after their Christmas celebrations.

December 27th it rained a little, but Red and I braved the weather and went out for a while in the afternoon. In the evening we saw a musical and vocal show in the mess hall, put on by the Y.M.C.A. It was a high class show and exceptionally good. The pianist was a celebrated French lady who won first prize in a competition at a conservatory of music in Paris.

December 28th was rainy. Red was sick and as I did not want to go out alone I decided to spend the day in the ward.

December 29th was rainy. We had to stay in whether we wanted to or not. The Y.M.C.A. gave us a concert in the mess hall in the evening which helped to pass the time.

December 30th and it is still raining. We are getting disgusted but as we have a pretty fair library now, with a lot of books and magazines, we pass the time reading, mostly.

December 31st and it's raining as usual. I called on the dentist and he worked on one of my teeth. A clown show was pulled off in our ward and the Red Cross girls gave us candy and nuts. If not for the Red Cross I don't know what we would do.

January 1st, 1919. The New Year's Day was fair. I did not feel like going out but Red went out and when he came back he reported a large crowd in Issoudun. This day was also a holiday in France and the people took advantage of the nice weather to be outdoors.
    We had in our ward a French volunteer nurse. She was very popular with the boys and we pooled our money and bought her a present that we gave her in the afternoon. She was much pleased with the gift.

January 2nd had nice weather. I consulted the dentist and had X-ray pictures taken of my teeth. At three o'clock all of us patients in the hospital were paid our monthly casual pay. This amounted to about seven or eight dollars a month. In the evening we had a band concert in the mess hall with dancing for those who felt able to dance.

January 3rd it is raining again but we went out anyway. I had another appointment with the dentist.

January 4th, same old story, rain. It is very lonesome in the hospital and we would rather get wet than to stay inside so we went uptown.

January 5th, Sunday. Weather still rainy. Red and I went out and treated ourselves to supper in a cafe. We had an argument as to who should order the eats as we were both rather far behind in our studies of the French language. Red finally agreed to do the talking, and upon entering the cafe he faced the girl in charge with these words: "Avez vous beaucoup de pomme de terre?" This completely exhausted his supply of French but it achieved the desired result and we got beaucoup potatoes for the small sum of ten francs, about two dollars. In the evening we had religious services in the mess hall.

January 6th was classification day. Every Monday the patients who were nearly healed went before a medical board to be classified for evacuation. Class A men were considered first class men and were, in most cases, sent back to their organizations. B, C, and D classes were moved to a hospital nearer a sea port. This day only A, B, and C classes were processed. No passes were issued on classification days as the doctors wanted the men available whenever they were needed.

On January 7th it was nice weather and we went down to the railroad station. Passing the newsstand I noticed a French paper with large headings announcing that Theodore Roosevelt had died. The French people admired Roosevelt very much as he had always been a friend of theirs.

January 8th had nice weather again. The dentist worked on my teeth and in the afternoon we went to the ammunition factory and looked it over. We were required to get passes before we could go inside. They were remodeling it into a stove factory, and had a large number of German prisoners working there. A bunch of women and girls were engaged in picking small pieces of old, corroded iron out of a large hill of dirt. It was necessary for them to shovel and move the entire amount of dirt and it was very hard work. They were dressed in bloomers and from a distance could not be told from men.

January 9th. Weather nice. We went out and had a long walk in the country. In the hospital we now had a recreation room that was quite homelike and we spent most of our time there. Miss Baker, the Red Cross girl in charge, had several canary birds in cages in the room. One of them died and in the evening some of the boys rigged up a surprise on Miss Baker. As we were sitting in the room reading and talking, in came two soldiers carrying a French flag, followed by two others carrying a stretcher on which were several lighted candles, a lot of flowers, and a small paper box with the remains of the bird. There was a large placard on which someone wrote the words 'our own bird'. Behind the stretcher came a procession of twenty soldiers marching in pairs. All the usual ceremonies of a funeral were gone through and it ended with taps and three shots fired. This was probably the first canary bird that had a military funeral.

January 10th. The weather was nice and I visited a French barber shop for a haircut.

January 11th. Still fair weather. I decided to have my picture taken and went to a shop where it was done. They enjoy a good patronage from the American soldiers.

Photo postcard of Robert in Issoudun, January 11th, 1919

Robert in Issoudun, January 11th, 1919

January 12th was fair weather and I had another long walk. This was Sunday so we had services in the recreation room in the evening.

January 13th was classification day and we could get no passes so we had to remain inside in spite of the nice weather.

January 14th. Weather still fair. The Red Cross ladies served coffee and doughnuts in the recreation room. In our ward was a fellow who was rather ignorant and not well liked by the rest of the boys. We suspected him of being either pro-German or just plain nuts. A French soldier used to come by our ward to sell or trade for tobacco souvenirs, and 'Nuts' and another boy named Goetz wanted the same article that the Frenchman was showing us. Goetz bought the souvenir and Nuts got angry and went out, returning in a short while with a heavy cane that he rapped Goetz over the head with several times, cutting great gashes in his scalp which made it necessary to have Goetz taken to the operation room and stitches were required to sew the wounds up. Feelings against Nuts run high for a long while, but as they were both cripples walking on canes and crutches, nothing was done to punish Nuts.

January 15th. It was very nice weather and a bunch of us went out to the countryside. We visited Balzac's château[30] and took several pictures there. It was one of the most beautiful places I have ever seen. We were issued cans of candy by the Red Cross in the evening and afterwards watched a moving picture show in the mess hall. Everybody that could walk attended these shows.

January 16th and the weather is nice again. The Red Cross served cocoa and doughnuts, and they were real homemade doughnuts, too. In the evening we had entertainment in the recreation room - Miss Victor of Pittsburgh sang songs.

January 17th and we still have nice weather. There was a band concert and a dance in the recreation room in the evening. The dances were very popular and the French girls in Issoudun came to the hospital to dance with us Americans.

January 18th. It was pretty chilly and all I did was go out and pick up my pictures that I had taken a few days previously.

January 19th. I was sick today with a very high fever and chills. I could not leave my bed and felt pretty miserable.

January 20th. I am still sick in bed and am not improving any. Today is classification day so no passes were given out, but that did not bother me any as I was too sick to make use of one.

January 21st. Weather is nice. I am feeling a little better but can't leave my bed. In the evening the officers have a dance in the recreation room. At these dances the privates are supposed to stay away.

January 22nd. Nice weather yet. We had a moving picture show in the evening and I was able to attend that.

January 23rd. Still nice weather. I felt better today. Red was classified last Monday and he and a bunch of men were transferred to Camp Aignan. He was put in B class. Red's real name is Charles Pittman, from Brunswick, Missouri. He was wounded in the Battle of the Marne quite severely. We had so far occupied Ward D, but we were now so few in the hospital that they moved us all to F Ward. This ward was not nearly as nice as D ward.

January 24th. Today is the coldest weather I have experienced in France. When we awoke this morning we saw traces of ice on the windows, but later in the day it got very nice.

January 25th. This was another cold day. A number of new patients from Laurent arrived at our hospital. The were all sick cases. In the evening we saw a very good moving picture show. After we retired for the night, the engine in the power plant exploded! The large wooden house which housed the power plant and the garage next to it caught fire and burned down. Ten large barrels of gasoline exploded, and it looked and sounded like the Battle of the Argonne. This building was connected with the hospital so we were in danger of getting burnt ourselves. Both the American and the French fire departments were called out but there was either something wrong with their hoses or else they decided to let the fire burn and they just kept it from spreading.

January 26th. Today it is snowing. This is the first snow I have seen in France. It snowed just enough to cover the ground. This is Sunday but for some reason they had a preliminary classification today. Captain Faucett conducted the review and he marked me C class. We had our usual divine services in the evening.

January 27th. This was the regular classification day. I was called up before the board and was again put in C class, this time for good as they never changed this.

January 28th. It was snowing again today. It was a real pretty snow. Large white flakes fell slowly until the ground got very white. The snow was wet and made the streets pretty slushy, so the officers decided that we could not get any passes. In the evening there was another dance.

January 29th. The weather was fair and we went out to look at some aeroplanes that were loaded on a train for shipment. Some of them had been in fights and showed marks of German bullets and shrapnel. They had a bunch of German prisoners working in a warehouse but they only loafed as long as we were there.

January 30th. It was nice weather and the snow melted quickly. This was a holiday for us and we were ordered to sign the payroll.

January 31st. I walked uptown and found everything very quiet. French soldiers are generally seen on the streets but they were gone today, too.

February 1st. Fair weather. We strolled down the streets and saw people bustling around the church so we went there to investigate and found that a double wedding was on the program. The first pair were a French soldier and a young girl, the other pair were a little older. The traditional Catholic wedding ceremonies were employed and it seemed to be quite a job to get married in France. We went back to the hospital and took in a minstrel show that was staged in the evening.

February 2nd. This was Sunday and the weather was cold. We had our services as usual.

February 3rd. This was classification day so we got no passes, and besides this it was payday. I got 59 francs, 95 centimes. Today I received my first letter from home since September! It was from my nephew Leroy Youngberg, dated November 4th. A dance was held in the evening.

February 4th. I received two more letters from home; one from dad dated November 4th, and another from Amanda dated December 16th. A and B class patients left for Camp Aignan. I walked through the park surrounding the hospital. They had a large number of statues and sculptural work. They also had a piece of the original cross, at least they claimed it to be genuine.

February 5th. I received a letter from Fridolf dated October 20th. It rained and I remained in the ward all day.

February 6th. Received three more letters from Amanda, Harold, and Esther. There was great rejoicing among the boys on account of rumors that we were going to leave the hospital in the afternoon. It proved to be a false alarm, though, and we were pretty blue for a long while.

February 7th. Raining again. Another false alarm was spread about our moving, but we were more skeptical now.

February 8th. It was cold today. At eleven o'clock we were ordered to get ready to leave Issoudun. A Red Cross train was coming to take all the patients that could be moved. As soon as the train arrived we went aboard. It was an American train and very comfortable. We traveled all night.

Beau Désert and Base Hospital #114

February 9th, Sunday. We arrived at Base Hospital #114, Beau Désert,[31] at six o'clock in the morning. It was very cold and we were shivering. We went to the receiving ward and were assigned to different wards. I went to Ward #13. Later in the day we were transferred to ward #44. This was nothing but a warehouse or magazine, but on account of a fire that occurred a few days prior to our arrival they had to utilize this for a ward because two wards burned down in the fire. It was very cold and we had a hard time keeping warm. In the afternoon we went to the Red Cross room and took in a show. It was very good.

When we came back to the ward we found four one-legged cripples trying to hold down another one-legged boy in the bed. He had a severe case of delirium tremens and as he was very violent and raging mad, it took all the strength of the men to hold him down. Towards evening he became so violent that he was moved to the insane ward and put in a straitjacket. He recovered and after a few days he came back to us.

February 10th. We had a hard time getting wood for the little stove in our large ward and we suffered quite a good deal from the cold. We went to a show in the evening. The Red Cross here at Beau Désert gave some very good shows, much better than we were used to.

February 11th. Pretty cold. The Americans had a large number of German prisoners and several thousand Chinese coolies working here. They were employed mostly in piling lumber and loading lumber on cars. The Chinese were dressed in old overalls and stuffed the legs and arms until they resembled rag dolls. They worked very slowly. The Germans were good workers and the more trusted were allowed to come and go pretty much as they pleased inside the camp limits. They kept the roads in repair and repaired windows, doors, and locks, etcetera. In the afternoon we went to a moving picture show.

February 12th. The weather was very nice and we walked around the hospital grounds. I went to the barber shop and had my hair cut.

February 13th. Weather still very nice. Quite a little excitement was created in the morning when a report came that the Germans had begun fighting again. We soon found out that it wasn't true. We went to a show in the evening.

February 14th. Raining today. I spent most of the day in my ward. I attended a party by the Red Cross in the evening. They served cocoa and cake and afterwards a show was held.

February 15th. Raining some more. I was transferred to ward #8 and as I and one other boy were the only walking patients in the ward, we had to help with the K.P. work. The work was very light; we carried the food from the kitchen to the ward and filled the plates for the bedridden patients. We also washed the dishes. In the evening we went to a show.

February 16th, Sunday. Weather was fair and we went to the Red Cross room where they had religious services. The chaplain gave a very good sermon. In the afternoon at one o'clock the 159th Infantry Band gave a good concert. At dinner we had a very agreeable surprise when we found pie on the bill of fare. In the evening I went to church again.

February 17th. It rained again. The ward surgeon examined me as that has to be done whenever a man is transferred from one ward to another. Went to a show in evening.

February 18th. It rained all day so I stayed in the ward and helped feed the patients.

February 19th. More rain. A number of new patients came to our ward. In the evening I went to a show.

February 20th. Still raining. I was transferred to ward #31. For some reason they continually moved us patients around from one ward to another and every time we moved we used to say that it was another step towards home. When the newspapers arrived we read that Clemenceau[32] was shot.

February 21st. It rained all day and we remained in our wards. We now stayed in the south end of the hospital, quite a distance from the Red Cross building.

February 22nd. Raining more. Today was Washington's Birthday and a Washington-themed show was performed in the Red Cross building. It was a very nice program and much enjoyed. In the afternoon the Whizz Bangs performed.[33] This was a play by a regiment and had a very good reputation. We learned today that Kurt Eisner, premier of Bavaria, was shot.[34]

February 23rd. Sunday. We took another step towards home and moved to ward #29. It rained all day and we had to stay inside.

February 24th. Same story again. It rained and we were kept in the ward. We are all getting very impatient because we can not go home.

February 25th. Once again it was rainy and cold. We heard a rumor about General Pershing coming to inspect us.

Beau Désert is a great American hospital center. It includes Base Hospitals numbers 11, 114, 121, and Evacuation Hospital #20. Located about ten miles east of Bordeaux on a great plain, it is in a very beautiful part of France. Barracks are used here, each barrack constituting a separate ward. The whole hospital center was laid out like a city with long straight streets and barracks on both sides, and board sidewalks which made it possible to keep everything clean and in good condition. Each hospital had about fifty wards or barracks and each barrack had about fifty beds. Each ward had a surgeon who was in charge of the ward, two nurses and two orderlies during the day, and one nurse and one orderly during the night. Every day there was an inspection of the wards. An officer, a major as a rule, would make daily rounds, inspecting everything. Some of them were pretty picky and they usually found something to complain about. Military discipline was very strict in the hospitals in France, but as we neared home it gradually loosened up and we got a bit more freedom.

February 26th. Another quiet day, it rained and was quite cold.

February 27th. Fair but blustery. Going to a moving picture was all I did today.

February 28th. Raining some more. We spent the time reading the papers and wishing that we could go home.

March 1st. Still raining. General Pershing came and inspected the hospital about noon. We assembled in the Red Cross building where he made a speech to us. He is a plain-speaking man, but every word he says counts. He expressed his thanks to all American soldiers for the great work they had done and their bravery and courage displayed in action. He was plainly dressed and wore no decorations of any kind. He was accompanied by two brigadier generals and several other officers. They traveled in automobiles. In the afternoon we were examined by a major in our ward. We had two examinations prior to being evacuated. In the evening we went to the picture show and saw the famous 'Sweetheart of the Doomed.'

Evacuation Hospital #20

March 2nd. This was Sunday and the weather was fair. We moved to Evacuation Hospital #20 which made us a happy bunch as we knew that the next move would be to our ship. We went through several examinations and our clothes were scrutinized closely. Those smitten by cooties took a thorough bath and were given clean clothes. More examinations came and then we were assigned to our wards. I was sent to ward #3 where we again were submitted to examinations by the ward surgeons. In the evening when everything was over, we went to a lecture by a Canadian officer, a former prisoner in Germany. He exposed a lot of German cruelties that were unknown even to us who had faced them on the field of battle. We moved all clocks ahead one hour today. This changing of time was never noticed by us in the hospitals.

March 3rd. Raining again. We were called together and a casual company was organized. We were hereafter to be Casual Company #156 in the charge of a sergeant, himself a patient in the hospital. This being completed, we had roll call and signed the payroll. Previously we were issued pay books and we were ordered to turn these in.

March 4th. They issued us whatever clothes we needed, extra underwear, two blankets, and toilet articles. Later in the day we were paid. I received $11.10, and good American money at that. We had an opportunity to exchange French currency for American at the rate of 5 francs 45 centimes per dollar. For my 307 francs I got $56.30 in return.

March 5th. We assembled for our final overseas examination. The all-important cootie exam of course came first. Same thing was gone through as the first time. Then came the different examinations of eyes, nose, throat, and so forth, followed by the best feature of the whole program; we were issued gangplank numbers! Mine was number 126. A last chance was given to those who wanted to exchange clothes that they were unable for some reason to wear.

8 THE LONG TRIP HOME

Bordeaux to New York City

March 6th. Roused out of bed at 3:30 A.M., we were served breakfast at 4:15. At 5:00 we were loaded into ambulances and driven to the harbor at Bordeaux. We made good time and soon were at the docks. The Red Cross gave us coffee and sandwiches while we waited to board the boat. About 6:00 we went aboard the USS Walter A. Luckenbach.[35] It was a small freight boat, 470 feet long and 56 feet wide. It was very crowded and uncomfortable but we did not mind as we were going home. We would have taken almost any ship rather than stay in France a day longer. We remained in the harbor until late in the evening, then pulled anchor and proceeded up the river until we came to a place where we had to wait for the tide before crossing a sand bar. I got up on deck about 8:00 the next morning and could no longer see the shores of France.

March 7th. It began to blow as soon as we got out on the open ocean, and kept getting worse. Accommodations on the ship were not very good. The Walter A. Luckenbach carried 2,250 casuals and about 350 wounded soldiers and we were pretty crowded. The system of feeding us was very poor. The food was carried down to us in the hatches, and as every space was taken up by the bunks we slept in, there was little room to eat. The men began to get seasick.

March 8th. The storm was getting worse, and almost everybody was more or less seasick. Most of us needed our wounds dressed daily; two lieutenants and a captain were in charge of us and did the dressing. The only place with room to do this was in the hatch where we slept and ate. Today they were all sick. The captain did not show up until late in the afternoon and the lieutenants were so sick that while they were attending the wounds they had to turn aside and vomit. I was feeling good myself and was quite hungry.

March 9th, Sunday. The sea was increasingly rough and the wind increasingly strong. Almost everybody was sick, but I was feeling good and was mostly enjoying myself. They held religious services on the ship but I did not know where.

March 10th. About 2:00 we ran into even worse weather. It stormed hard but I was still feeling fine.

March 11th. The stormy sea continues without any letup. About noon we passed an ocean liner and a sailboat, both going in the same direction as we were. We were puzzled how a sailboat could hold it's own in a sea like this. I was feeling fine.

March 12. There is no letup in the storm. At 1:00 we had medical inspection on the ship. About 6:00 in the evening we met a large passenger boat and she was also hard pressed by the storm. I felt good as usual.

March 13th. We were now in a regular hurricane! For the last few days the waves swept over the deck and water ran down into the hatches onto our beds, forcing some of us to leave them. The ship rocked and pitched so hard that the bunk in hatch B3 below us caved in, injuring several men. I was not seasick, but I was badly scared, as were the rest of the men.

March 14th. The sea is still rough and it has turned cold. I am feeling good but it is uncomfortable to be up on deck.

March 15th. The storm has abated some but it is bitterly cold and snowing. It is so cold that the only way we can keep warm is to lie in our beds and cover ourselves up. We had to declare everything we brought with us from France as we have to pay duty on anything above $100 worth of personal property. I continue to feel good.

March 16th, Sunday. The storm has finally ceased and it is not blowing very hard. Now, however, our engine stopped working, and we drifted from 1:00 to 10:00 P.M. Most of us are feeling good but pretty impatient at the delay.

March 17th. This was St. Patrick's Day. The seas were fair but it was very foggy. We had to stop once again on account of engine trouble and had to drift. We met two boats and had our first and only lifeboat drill of the trip. I was in the best of health.

March 18th. It was very foggy in the morning and it rained hard. They sounded the water depth continually. About 12:00 the fog suddenly lifted and we saw land in the distance which might have been the shores of New Jersey. About 1:00 the harbor pilot boarded our ship and we sailed to the dock in New York Harbor and remained there for the night.

New York City

March 19th. We got off the boat at 10:00 in the morning and went on a ferry where we were served a good meal. When we landed, we were loaded into ambulances and taken to Debarkation Hospital #5 at Grand Central Palace[36] on the corner of 47th Street and Lexington Avenue. When we arrived there everything was taken away from us. After a hot bath they gave us pajamas and jackets and treated us to another feed, which convinced us that we were in the U.S. of A. sure enough, then they took us to ward 4C.

March 20th. We had no clothes so we just loafed and went to the theater in the hospital where a large chorus sang a welcome to us.

March 21st. We got our clothes and went out sightseeing. We got passes every day from noon to midnight. I just walked around today.

March 22nd. We walked around all over the city. We all were tickled silly at being back in the States once more! I had been gone ten months and a half.

March 23rd, Sunday. The wife of a senator took us out sightseeing in a Red Cross bus. We visited Grant's tomb and saw the residences of Carnegie, Astor, Vanderbilt, Morgan, and many other millionaires' homes. We also had a swell feed.

March 24th. The Knights of Columbus took us out today and showed us New York. We saw the church where Washington worshipped and the home of President Monroe and the house in which the Monroe Doctrine was drawn. We drove along Canal street where Fulton experimented with his steamboat which was then part of the Hudson river but now everything around it is built up and looks like any other part of New York. We saw the residences of the inventor of Pepsin gum and Schwab and Clark, then we visited Castle Garden where Jenny Lind sang and where so many were injured in the large crowd. This is now a museum where they keep rare species of fish. When I returned to my ward I found two telegrams from home announcing John's death.[37]

March 25th. The 27th Division paraded today. I had a good seat in a window of a beautiful house on Fifth Avenue. In the evening I went to Madison Square Roof Garden where Thaw shot White.[38]

March 26th. The popular actress Mae Sims gave a banquet for us today. It was rather high-toned but we got through it all right. In the evening I took in the entertainment in the assembly room and that was very good.

March 27th. I went to the Hall of States and met Mrs. Colonel White[39] of Valley City and Miss Wenberg of Beach, N.D. I was invited to a banquet by the Women's Apparel Association. This was a very swell affair. After the banquet Miss Bernstein, who was in charge, gave us tickets to the casino where the play 'Some Time' was put on. The tickets were worth $2.00.

March 28th we were entertained by the Château Thierry Club in the afternoon. In the evening Miss Rice of Edison and Victor record fame[40] and Phillips the tenor sang for us. This was real classy stuff.

March 29th. It was very stormy and cold today so when I was offered a $2.00 ticket to the Century Theater on 61st Street and Broadway I took it. The 27th Division gave their play, 'Lets Beat It.'

March 30th, Sunday. We were given tickets to the Manhattan Opera House and I went there and saw a good play.

Fort Snelling in Minneapolis

March 31st. We left New York City in the morning at 9:00 on the Pennsy railroad.[41] We passed through Philadelphia about noon and reached Harrisburg about 10:00 PM. We got to Pittsburgh at 2:00 AM.

April 1st. We passed through Canton and the rest of Ohio and got to Fort Wayne, Indiana about 10:00. We arrived in

Chicago around 6:00 in the evening. Our car was taken to a repair track and a new set of wheels put on. From there we went on the Chicago, Milwaukee & St. Paul Railroad and came to Milwaukee about 8:00 PM.

April 2nd. We arrived in Minneapolis at 6:00 in the morning and we rode in automobiles to Fort Snelling, or General Hospital #29. I got a pass and went to Arvid Lindquist's home for supper. I also went to Emil's shop and was measured for a suit.

April 3rd. When I arrived at Fort Snelling I was assigned to ward 3B North. The hospital consisted of old barracks that formerly housed soldiers stationed here. The officers were quartered in barracks on the opposite side of the street. They had a large force of doctors, nurses, and Red Cross workers, plus many schools and shops where the disabled soldiers were taught new occupations. Colonel Gentry was in charge of the post; Captain Jones was our ward surgeon.

At Fort Snelling we could only get passes to leave the hospital on Wednesdays, Saturdays, and Sundays, so in the evening we went to the Knights of Columbus room and gymnasium where they pulled off some mighty good boxing bouts. They had several but the best one was the main event, six rounds between a man named Jack and his adversary, Young Kellerman.

April 4th. This was a quiet, lonesome day. We had just arrived from New York City where there was something doing all the time, and here we could not even get passes to go out. In the evening we were entertained by the street car girls of Minneapolis. They sang for us and afterwards we played games. Most important of all we were served a big feed, which appealed highly to all of us.

April 5th. Today I went to Minneapolis as this was one of the few pass days. The street car line was just a few blocks from the hospital.

April 6th, Sunday. I went to the tabernacle and heard Hjerpe speak.[42] The rest of the day I spent with Emil and his family in the city.

April 7th. One of the rules in the hospital was that every patient had to be out of bed, if he was able, before nine o'clock. The sergeant in charge came around every morning and called the roll. This morning Captain Jones himself came in and when I awoke he was standing over me and wanted to know the reason I was in bed this time of the day. I could give no good excuse so he told the sergeant to take my name. The punishment for this offense was loss of pass privileges for ten days. I expected to get punished, but they must have forgotten, and I got my pass when I applied for it the following pass day. Effie came to see me today.

April 8th. It was rainy and cold and disagreeable. The Red Cross has a very pretty building here at Fort Snelling. It was the most homelike place we had seen so far and it was for the exclusive use of wounded overseas patients only. No others were allowed in there. We had all the books and papers and magazines we could read, and almost every day visitors delivered candy, cakes, coffee and doughnuts. Tonight we had a program in the Red Cross building given by some of the players of the Metropolitan Opera House and it was greatly appreciated.

April 9th. Pass day again. I went to Minneapolis and had the tailor and watchmaker do some work for me. Afterwards I went to Emil's house.

April 10th. This was another rainy day so we all stayed inside. In the evening we went to the Red Cross and saw William Hart in 'The Cold Deck' and also a couple reels of Fatty Arbuckle.[43]

April 11th. Pretty chilly today. We were paid in the afternoon. I received $25, the most money I had earned in a long while. We went to the Y.M.C.A. hut in the evening and saw another moving picture show.

April 12th. This was a very nice day so I went to Minneapolis and hunted up some friends that I had not seen for a long time.

April 13th, Sunday. I went to Elim Church in the forenoon with Emil's kids and spent the rest of the day at his house.

April 14th. Pretty bad weather today. It was snowing to beat the cards. I was called up before the disability board, consisting mostly of a major who examined our wounds and made a description or diagnosis of it. In the evening we saw another show in the Red Cross building.

April 15th. It was still snowing very hard. There are three places - the Red Cross, the Y.M.C.A., and the Knights of Columbus - where they entertain us almost every night. As a rule refreshments are served after the program is over, and we made it our business to find out where the best feed was to be had and went there without exception. There was not enough room in a single place for all the patients, so late arrivals had to go to the other two venues. We heard that the Red Cross was putting on a fair feed tonight so we went there.

April 16th. It was pass day so I went to Minneapolis and roamed around with friends. I went to Emil's shop and later to Arvid and Freda Lindquist's place at 3449 5th Avenue South. John Lindquist was 5 years old today.

April 17th. The weather was pretty fair today. In the evening I went to the Knights of Columbus boxing event. There was a cracking good bout between Sergeant Brown of the Fort Snelling Medical Corps and Joe Walch of the 125th Field

Artillery who had just arrived from France. It was a ten round bout and a fight from the minute it started until the last bell. Brown was the better fighter, but he seemed to lack the punch and was badly punished by Walch, who nearly won by a knockout.

April 18th. The weather was fair. General Wood[44] inspected our hospital and later in the day spoke in an auditorium in Minneapolis. Passes were given out to those who wished to go, but when we learned that we would have to go in special chartered cars and come home right afterwards the same way, we turned them down.

April 19th. A Liberty Loan parade was staged in the Twin Cities and private cars came to the hospital to get the soldiers who wanted to take part. On account of this we could not get our passes until four o'clock. When we got them I went to Emil's house.

April 20th was Easter Sunday. I went to the tabernacle and heard Johnson, then I spent the day with Emil's family.

April 21st was a great day at Fort Snelling. A program of exhibition flying was given which included sham battles between Allied and enemy planes. A large crowd from Minneapolis and St. Paul watched the exhibitions.

April 22nd. The Jewish Welfare Board[45] put on some good entertainment in the evening. The Jewish Welfare became famous at Fort Snelling through their royal treatment of us soldiers and the splendid shows and big feeds they gave us. Whenever they entertained, there was no question where to go. My wound healed shut today.

April 23rd. I went to a dentist in Minneapolis and he started working on my teeth. The rest of the day I visited friends in the city.

April 24th. I asked for a special pass to fulfill my engagement with my dentist, which was granted. I took advantage of the extra time to do some more visiting.

April 25th. I asked again for a special pass to see the dentist and also called on some of the folks.

April 26th. The dentist finished his work and I attended a little party later in the evening at Bergerman's on Portland and 16th Street.

April 27th, Sunday. It was cloudy and looked like rain. I went to Minneapolis and attended services in the Park Avenue Church.[46] The rest of the day I called on some friends.

April 28th. Today was a very nice day. I walked to the school and practiced a little on a Burroughs adding and calculation machine.[47]

April 29th. It was a very quiet day. I spent the evening at the Knights of Columbus show.

April 30th. I went to Minneapolis, visiting friends and walking around.

May 1st. The Jewish Welfare hosted entertainment in the Red Cross building. At the conclusion of the program Fred Fulton[48] was introduced to us on the stage and received a splendid ovation. He made a short speech.

May 2nd. It was pretty quiet again. I began taking lessons in salesmanship as there was nothing else to do.

May 3rd. I went to Emil's house in Minneapolis for supper. I had a good time.

May 4th, Sunday. I went to services at the Park Avenue Church in the morning, then to the Johnson's house at 3705

24th Avenue for dinner and supper. We all went to St. John's Church in the evening.

May 5th. Today was a very disagreeable day, cold and rainy. Nothing doing except a show in the Red Cross building.

Free At Last

May 6th. We were called to the post chapel in the morning where we were instructed about a lot of subjects relative to getting our discharge. The man in charge was a government official and explained in particular the insurance; how to keep it up and what policy to take out, etcetera. In the afternoon they called me to the personnel office and wanted my life's history. Apparently this was necessary in order to make out my discharge. In the evening we attended another show by the Jewish Welfare.

May 7th. I turned in all my extra clothing, and the little red chevron I coveted so much was issued to me.[49] In the afternoon I went to Emil's house.

May 8th. Today was the day of the big parades. At nine o'clock automobiles came to the hospital and took us to St. Paul, where we paraded through the main part of the city in the forenoon. After the parade they took us to the Elks Club for a banquet. We had a swell dinner and there was singing during the whole meal. After dinner we listened to speeches and the speakers praised us hugely. We then went back to Fort Snelling the same way we left it, stepped into the Minneapolis cars that were waiting for us, and proceeded to our second parade. This parade started at Midway and proceeded down Nicollet Avenue to the parade grounds at the Armory, where speeches and other things were indulged in. We passed through throngs of people, massed as thick as they could squeeze themselves together. It was estimated that 300,000 people in Minneapolis were at the parade. I made my way back to the hospital after the parade, where I learned that the lid was taken off for the day and we could come and go as we pleased without passes, so I went back to the city.

May 9th. Another rainy, disagreeable day, we spent most of it inside, resting from the strenuous day before.

May 10th. We had nice weather today. I was called to the vocational board, where disabled soldiers are instructed in their ability to make a living in the future. Those who cannot follow their former occupations are helped in choosing another and the government teaches them if necessary. In the afternoon I went to Minneapolis, feeling pretty good about soon being out of the army.

May 11th, Sunday. I went, as usual, to Minneapolis and spent some time with the folks.

May 12th. This was the biggest day of them all; I was discharged! Before discharge, however, I had to be paid. I was not notified about this and missed the chance in the morning when most of the others were paid in the canteen. After considerable trouble I located the quartermaster's place a mile from the hospital and was fixed up. I got my little old paper that said I was free!

I arrived home on May 17th, 1919, after being gone for one year, one month, and twenty days. I had been in the United States Army for one year, one month, and thirteen days.

Private Robert Waldemar Safstrom

NOTES

1. Probably refers to the R.M.S. Missanabie, a Canadian ocean liner used to transport troops across the Atlantic in the Great War. Struck by torpedoes from the German U-87 submarine, it sunk 52 miles off the coast of Ireland on September 9th, 1918 on it's return trip from Liverpool to New York City.
2. The R.M.S. Olympic, a British luxury passenger ship similar to her sister, the Titanic, was refitted in 1915 and converted for troop transport.
3. 'Hommes 40 Chevaux 8' translated to English means 'Men 40 Horses 8', the load limits for the rail car.
4. Major General William M. Wright, 1863-1943, commander of the 35th Division, among others, during the Great War.
5. Eddystone Arsenal, a division of Remington, manufactured the M1917 Enfield rifle in Eddystone, Pennsylvania. It was a modified version of the British .303 Enfield, altered to fire the U.S. standard .30-06 cartridge. Bolt action, with a 6 round magazine that was reloaded with 5 round clips, it weighed 11 pounds with a bayonet.
6. Hard tack, or hardtack, is a simple, long-lasting mix of flour, water, and salt baked into a hard biscuit. Corn willy, with various spellings, is slang for corned beef.
7. Boche is a derogatory French slang word for German.
8. Canadian physician and Lieutenant Colonel John McCrae wrote *In Flanders Fields* (public domain) in 1915 following the funeral of a friend who died in battle during World War I. The poem, used during the war for propaganda and marketing war bonds, is especially popular in Canada. Our current use of the poppy to memorialize soldiers who died in battle is derived from this poem. McCrae, worn down by the war, died of cerebral meningitis in a military hospital in Wimereux, France, January 28, 1918, six months before Private Safstrom marched to the front.
9. Hartmannswillerkopf overlooks the plain of Alsace, and was the scene of intense battles starting in 1914. By the

time Private Safstrom arrived it looked like a lunar landscape from all the shelling. It is now the site of one of four World War I national monuments in France.
10. A minenwerfer (German for 'mine launcher') was a portable, short-range mortar with an explosive shell used extensively along the trenches.
11. Joseph Pirkl, born December 14th, 1888 in Owatonna, Minnesota, lived in McLean County, North Dakota, and was inducted into the army March 28, 1918. He went to Camp Dodge, Iowa, and was in the 163rd Depot Brigade prior to transfer to Company L, 138th Infantry. He was killed in action July 11th, 1918, France, and is buried in the Meuse-Argonne American Cemetery, Romagne, France; Block D, Row 26, Grave 22.
12. American Expeditionary Force, a synonym for the American Armed Forces sent to Europe during World War I.
13. Alexander Rives Seamon, born January 28th, 1890. First Lieutenant, US Army 138th Infantry Regiment, 35th Infantry Division. He was killed in action September 29, 1918 in France, and is buried in the Meuse-Argonne American Cemetery, Romagne, France; Block A, Row 46, Grave 38.
14. The Saint-Mihiel Offensive, led by General Pershing, was the first wholly-American effort in the war. Earlier fighting was combined with French and British troops. When the United States joined the war effort, the British and French wanted us to join their forces as replacements, but Pershing fought to keep the A.E.F. a separate force under his command. Salient refers to the projecting angle of land where the German lines indented the Allied territory.
15. The region of the Argonne Forest, in the far north east of France. The Argonne Offensive, Meuse-Argonne Offensive, and Battle of the Argonne Forest all refer to the same area.
16. A macadam road is one made of uniformly sized gravel held together with a binding agent. It was developed by John McAdam.
17. Clermont-en-Argonne, for clarification.

18. These distance estimates are a bit high. 22 miles northwest of Verdun and 4 miles south of Varennes is more accurate.
19. Chlorine, phosgene, and mustard gases were used in World War I.
20. Ferdinand Foch (Fōsh), 1851-1929, appointed Marshal of France, was the Allied Supreme Commander.
21. General John Joseph 'Black Jack' Pershing, 1860-1948, led the American Expeditionary Forces. He was known for his disdain of trench warfare and his willingness to sacrifice soldiers in frontal charges. His nickname came from his time commanding the 10th Cavalry Regiment, the segregated African-American soldiers, also known as the 'Buffalo Soldiers', in the Indian wars and later in Cuba during the Spanish-American War.
22. Friedrich Wilhelm Victor August Ernst, 1882-1951, last Crown Prince of the Kingdom of Prussia and the German Empire, son of Kaiser Wilhelm II.
23. The American Red Cross provided 4,800 ambulance drivers and 18,000 nurses as well as other medical services and entertainment to the A.E.F. during the war.
24. The Young Men's Christian Association fielded 26,000 paid staff and 35,000 volunteers to aid the war effort. The Y.M.C.A. provided 90% of the welfare work for the A.E.F, including shelter, food, mental and social services, entertainment, and aid to prisoners of war on both sides of the conflict.
25. Organized at the University of Maryland in Baltimore, Base Hospital #42 set up alongside several already established hospitals in Bazoilles-sur-Meuse, France, in the middle of July, 1918. It was designated as a special hospital for maxillofacial cases. With a normal capacity of 1,000 beds, it was expanded via tents to 2,000. During it's service, from July 1918 to January 1919, it treated 2,600 surgical patients and 4,600 medical patients.
26. Major Carey B. Gamble, M.C., Chief of Medicine, Base Hospital #42. M.C. stands for Medical Corps, and only M.D. or D.O. officers were in the Corps.

27. Lieutenant Colonel Archibald C. Harrison, M.C., Chief of Surgery and Commanding Officer, Base Hospital #42, August 20,1918 to May 2, 1919.
28. Camp Hospital #59 was a 600 bed hospital previously used by the French as such, but originally it was the École Sacré Coeur, a school for boys. A large, five story building with a surrounding park, it was ill-equipped for medical use and required extensive conversion.
29. The Issoudun Aerodrome, at the time the largest air base in the world, was home to the 3rd Aviation Instruction Center. At it's peak it had 13 air fields and 10,000 ground personnel. Gervais Raoul Lufberry, 1885-1918, was a French-American flying ace with 17 victories. He died in combat. Quentin Roosevelt, 1897-1918, President Theodore Roosevelt's youngest son, was shot down, mortally wounded, behind German lines.
30. Château de Frapesle, in Issoudun, where the famous French author Honoré de Balzac often stayed.
31. Beau Désert, Mérignac, Department Gironde, France. Base Hospital #114 was a large, 5,000 bed hospital in Bordeaux on the west coast. Following the Armistice it functioned as an evacuation hospital for orthopedic patients.
32. Georges Benjamin Clemenceau, 1841-1929, statesman and Prime Minister of France, was one of the architects of the treaty of Versailles. A failed assassination attempt happened on February 19th, 1919.
33. The Whizz-Bangs were an entertainment troupe from Great Britain, operating as part of the Gloucestershire Regiment.
34. Kurt Eisner, a German politician and anti-war journalist of Jewish decent with a communist philosophy, was a lightning rod in his home country. He was shot and killed by a German nationalist February 21st, 1919 in Munich. Ironically, Adolf Hitler attended his funeral.
35. The USS Walter A. Luckenbach, built in Seattle, Washington and initially used as a naval cargo ship, was converted to troop transport by January, 1919. She made

five round trip voyages to France for this purpose before being decommissioned and returned to private ownership.
36. Grand Central Palace, an exhibition hall in New York City, was razed in 1964.
37. Private Safstrom's older brother John, a minister in the Congregational Church of Gwinner, ND, died of a lingering illness March 23, 1919.
38. At the Roof Garden Theater of Madison Square Garden, June 25, 1906, architect Stanford White was murdered by millionaire Harry Thaw for an affair that White had with Thaw's wife, actress Evelyn Nesbit.
39. Frank White, 1856-1940, served as a major with the ND Volunteer Infantry in the Philippines during the Spanish-American War. He was made a colonel for service in France during World War I, but did not serve in combat due to his age. Born in IL, lived in ND, and died in Washington, D.C., he was ND's 8th governor, 1901-1905, and the Treasurer of the United States from 1921-1928.
40. Gladys Rice, 1890-1983, was a popular American singer who recorded music for Edison starting around 1910.
41. The Pennsylvania Railroad
42. Most likely refers to the Swedish Tabernacle in Minneapolis, and Erik Gustaf Hjerpe, 1853-1931, president of the Covenant Evangelical Church of America.
43. William S. Hart, 1864-1946, was an American silent film actor whose career was fading by the time he made 'The Cold Deck' in 1917. Roscoe 'Fatty' Arbuckle, 1887-1933, was a talented comedian and silent film actor who discovered Bob Hope and Buster Keaton and mentored Charlie Chaplin. He is largely forgotten due the scandal of his two mistrials and later acquittal on the charges of rape and murder of aspiring actress Virginia Rappe.
44. General Leonard Wood, 1860-1927, namesake of Fort Leonard Wood in MO, was a physician, Medal of Honor recipient, and Army Chief of Staff.
45. The National Jewish Welfare Board was formed in 1917 to support Jewish soldiers in World War I.

46. Park Avenue Methodist Church, 3400 Park Avenue South, Minneapolis.
47. William Seward Burroughs perfected the mechanical adding machine and founded the company bearing his name. A relatively recent invention, Private Safstrom probably hadn't seen one before, but would have great interest in it due to his profession.
48. Fred Tobias Fulton or 'The Rochester Plasterer', 1891-1973, was a 6 foot 6 inch tall, left-handed heavyweight boxer who lived in Minnesota.
49. This red chevron, or honorable discharge stripe, was sewn onto the left sleeve halfway between the shoulder and elbow. It allowed the soldier to continue wearing his uniform after discharge.

PHOTOGRAPHS

Safstrom family circa 1903
Back row, left to right: Robert, Hulda, John, Amanda, Fridolf
Front row: Anna Marie, Hilding, Andrew

Robert and his wife Rose

Top: Robert and Rose with children, 1950s
Bottom: Sargent County Auditor's Office, 1923
Robert is second from the left

Robert playing the accordion

LETTERS TO HOME

Camp Dodge, Iowa, March 31st

Dear Folks:

Arrived here safely and had quite a trip. Our train had eleven coaches when we got into Minneapolis. About 500 men and everybody treated like kings instead of ordinary mortals.

The Red Cross at Hankinson served us a big lunch. We got into Minneapolis at six o'clock in the morning and had a swell breakfast at the Arcades. The next meal, dinner, was served in the dining car and supper at Ames, Iowa. And what a meal! Meat, pie, ice cream, and a whole lot more than we could eat. While enjoying the meal a big choir was singing, bands were playing, and people were singing and cheering for us all the way from Forman to Camp Dodge.

We got into camp about twelve o'clock Saturday night, not getting into bed until four o'clock, and were up again at six. We are now quarantined for two weeks. All Sargent and Wells County men are in this place. Jack Dyste was our captain in charge on the trip. I have not seen Hilding yet. I know about six or eight of the fellows are here. Saw Ralph Van Lear this morning.

The Y.M.C.A. is doing splendid work here. They have a man on every troop train to look after the comfort of the boys.

Kind greetings to all.

Robert

Co. Q, 163rd Depot Brigade
4th Battalion, Camp Dodge

Issoudun, November 24th, 1918

Dear Father:

Father's Day, so I am writing a letter like all the rest. I don't know what to write. Perhaps I should say something about the battle in which I was wounded.

We went into the front line trenches about midnight, the 25th of September, and about that time our artillery started the bombardment, which has never been equalled. This was kept up until noon the following day. The zero hour was set at five-thirty as near as I can remember and exactly at that time we went over the top, beginning the drive that ended the war.

I cannot give you the exact position we occupied as I had no map, but at a rough guess we were about fifty miles northwest of Verdun. Everything went fine. The Boches did not feel much like fighting and in most cases it was 'Kamerad'. We gathered in a goodly bunch of prisoners. I don't know just how many but I know that our company captured more prisoners than we were men in the company. In the afternoon the enemy opened up a heavy artillery fire and one shell got me.

I am getting along very nicely. Am up and around most of the time. Am sending pictures of the hospital I am in. Issoudun is a town of about 14,000 inhabitants. You will find it on the map I think about 100 miles south of Paris.

Merry Christmas and Happy New Year,

Pvt. R.W. Safstrom
Co. M, 188th Inf., A.E.F.

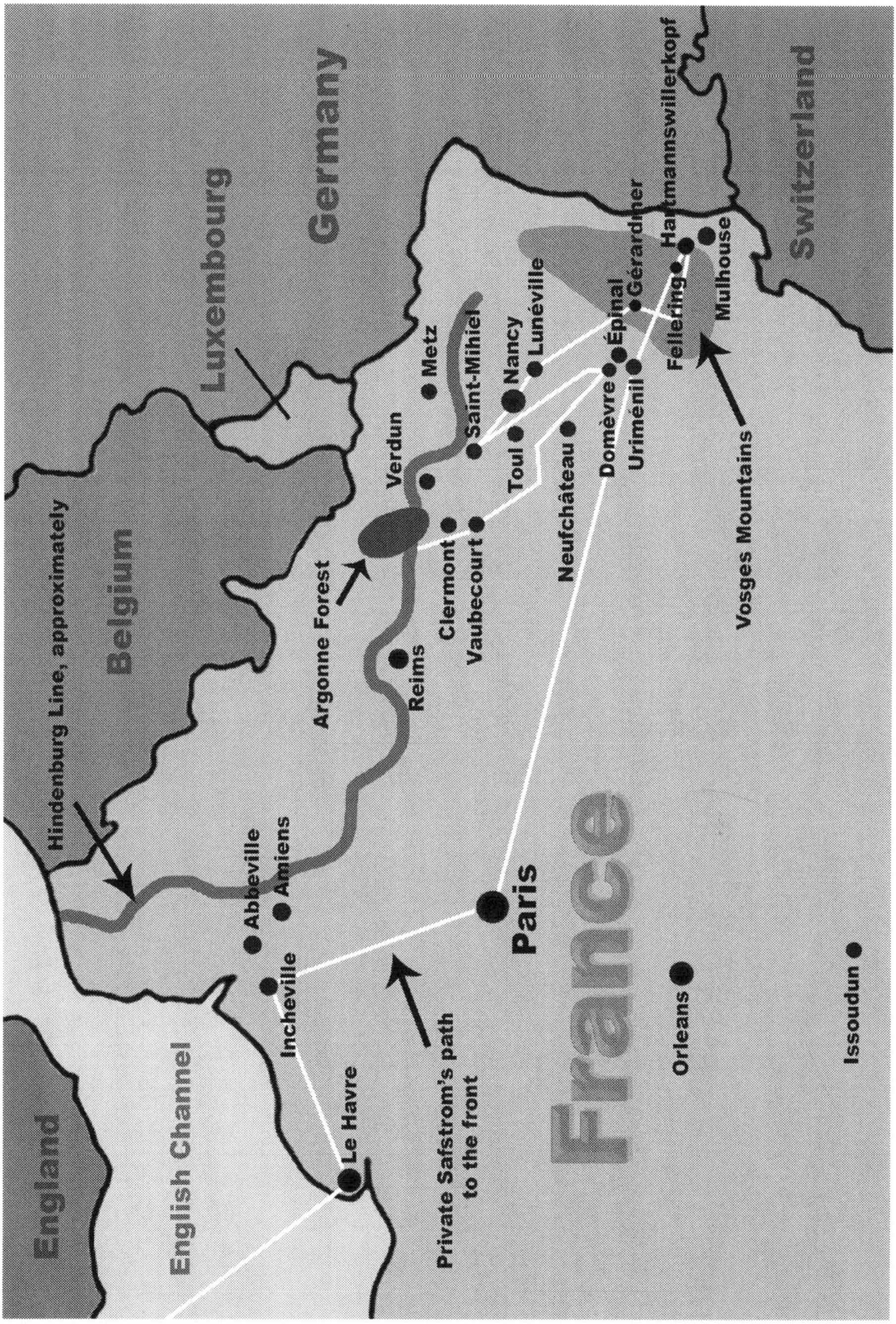
England
English Channel
Le Havre
Incheville
Abbeville
Amiens
Private Safstrom's path
to the front
Paris
France
Orleans
Issoudun
Hindenburg Line, approximately
Belgium
Luxembourg
Germany
Argonne Forest
Reims
Clermont
Vaubecourt
Verdun
Metz
Saint-Mihiel
Toul
Nancy
Lunéville
Neufchâteau
Domèvre
Uriménil
Épinal
Gérardmer
Fellering
Hartmannswillerkopf
Mulhouse
Vosges Mountains
Switzerland

Sample pages from the 6.75 x 4.25 inch diary,
written mostly in fading pencil and in small script.

About the Author

Chad R. Justesen, MD is a North Dakota native, a retired neurosurgeon, and lives with his wife Shawn in Fargo.

Made in the USA
Lexington, KY
08 June 2017